NIGERIA

DR. KEMDI CHINO OPARA

BookSide Press
877-741-8091
www.booksidepress.com
orders@booksidepress.com

Contents

PREFACE

In many public meetings and campaign appearances with constituent members in various parts of the local government areas during my twenty-plus-year-old political career, it is very evident that many people do not have a clue of how the National Assembly functions and what actually their representatives are required to do to enhance their daily lives as well as ways they can serve them better. In other words, accountability has always been a missing link between the *servant leader* and the *served*.

Constituent members often voiced out or better yet made utterances that had no bearing with what the functions of the National Assembly should be. Many a time, I was put in a position to lecture and correct some notions. Many people did not know that the National Assembly is the very "first arm" of the Federal Republic of Nigeria. It is Nigeria's bicameral legislature and the highest lawmaking body of the nation. It consists of the 109-member Senate and the 360-member House of Representatives. The term of office is four years from the date of its first sitting immediately after the general elections. This lawmaking function is one of the most essential pillars of any nation and must be taken seriously. In a democratic environment, power belongs to the people, who in turn elect those who are to carry out the important task of lawmaking on their behalf. Our welfare depends on the laws they make. It is important to know that this branch of government is set up or designed to address the needs, aspirations, and most importantly, the desires of the populace through lawmaking.

If our democracy is x-rayed to reveal its dysfunctionality that has left a vast majority of the populace with great sense of disquiet, the naked truth then becomes that the National Assembly has not functioned as it should. There has been a big disconnect between the elected officials and the governed. The beliefs of the governed are that the elected officials are often not voted in by them, and most, if not all, are there for personal gains and not for the interest of the populace. To put it in a better perspective, the officials (elected) or (selected) are unresponsive and irrelevant. The governmental system as presidential in style as it might seem did not quite model a system of representative democracy, which, in all sense of it, is not, according to the populace, both the alienable right and responsibility to become involved in governance.

As a consecutive four-time candidate for the position of Federal House of Representative and a current aspirant for the senatorial seat in Imo State, I have continued to work, inform, and educate as well as shed new light on the role of the National Assembly in our great republic and ways we can begin to hold our *public officials* or *servant leaders* accountable. I believe that an informed voter will make informed decision(s). If voters are schooled properly on what the National Assembly does and what they should expect of their representatives, the great divide will then be a thing of the past. Now that we are attempting to have people's votes count during elections, the populace will then begin to have better representation. The voter's rights will be affirmed, and power to elect members of the National Assembly will be shifted from the "godfathers" to the "people."

My desire to write this book was born out of the deep belief in educating my Owerri zone federal constituency as well as other constituencies in Nigeria about the National Assembly and ways the populace can participate effectively in governance.

Finally, it is the insistence of my children, Kemdi Jr., Chibuzo, Chinwendu, and Ugochinyere, and mostly my darling wife, Angela, who made me commit my analysis of the National Assembly to writing and share such with the populace. My parents, Louis and Christiana, siblings, in-laws, Adila Slaughter and Chinyere Ogekalu, friends too numerous to mention provided great insights and encouraged me all the way to the realization of this project.

With great hope, it is my wish that these thoughts on National Assembly will contribute somehow to enhance our public understanding of our democracy.

Chapter 1

Brief History on the Nigerian "National Assembly"

The history of Nigeria's legislature predates the nation's political independence by a century. Sequel to the annexation of the coastal city of Lagos in 1861, a ten-man legislative council was constituted and inaugurated by the British colonialists on March 13, 1862. And following the annexation of the whole of Southern Nigeria in later years and its unification with the Lagos colony in 1906, the legislative council was empowered to make laws for the entire colony of Lagos and southern part of what is presently known as the Nigerian nation.

In 1914, the southern protectorate was unified with the then northern protectorate. In spite of this, both political entities continued to be governed by separate legislative bodies, until 1946 when the newly promulgated Richard's Constitution, made provisions for a Central Nigeria legislative council—a sort of National Assembly. It also made provisions for the establishment of regional legislative councils, known as House of Assembly, with the principal function of presenting nominees for the central legislative bodies. Five years later, a new constitution was promulgated, which gave the regional houses of assemblies the authority on certain matters. This was replaced in 1954 by the Lylleton Constitution, which for the first time provided for the residual, exclusive, and the concurrent lists, and defined spheres of powers between the central and regional legislative houses.

The independence constitution of 1960, made provisions for a bicameral legislature at the center made up of a forty-four-member Senate and a 305-member House of Representatives. The republican constitution of 1963 increased the membership strength of these houses to 312 for the House of Representatives and fifty-six for the Senate.

The legislature was one of the causalities of Nigeria's first military rule, which spanned from January 17, 1966, to October 1, 1976. During this period, most democratic structures, prominent among was the legislature, were abolished, while the military rulers operated a unilateral system of government.

The second republic was ushered in on October 1, 1979, through a groundwork prepared by a constitution drafting committee and a constituent assembly. These two bodies functioned between 1978 and 1979. They produced the constitution of the Federal Republic of Nigeria in 1979.

This constitution provided for an executive presidential system government, whose features include separation of powers among the three arms of government, viz. the executive, legislative, and judiciary. The second republic legislature was also bicameral. There was a Senate, with a membership strength of ninety-five (each of the then nineteen states in the country produced five senators) and a Federal House of Representatives with a membership strength of 450. The second republic was abruptly terminated by a military coup on December 31, 1983.

The third republic took off via a transition programmed midwife in 1985 by the military president Ibrahim Babangida's administration. The imposed transition program resulted in the election of ninety-one senators to the National Assembly in December 1992, with each of the then thirty states producing three senators and the Federal Capital Territory producing a seat. The Federal House of Representatives, however, had membership strength of 593; the seats were filled on the basis of one representative per each of the 593 local governments existing then in the country.

The annulment of the June 12, 1993, presidential election and the resulting political crisis thereof, led to the overthrow of the pseudo democratic government led then by Chief Earnest Shonekan on November 17, 1993. Nigeria did not witness democracy again until May 29, 1999, when the General Abdulsalam Abubakar military junta handed over to a democratically elected government under the leadership of President Olusegun Obasanjo.

This fourth republic was anchored on the 1999 Constitution, whose features are not substantially different from the 1979 Constitution. It provides for a bicameral legislature—the Senate and the Federal House of Representatives. The former is composed of 109 members, three each from the thirty-six states in the country, while the latter is composed of 360 members representing federal constituencies on an almost equal population basis.

For the first time in independent Nigeria, the National Assembly has endured for two full sessions of eight years and achieved uninterrupted legislative activities from 1999 to 2003 and from 2003 to 2007. Given its prior broken history, this is a remarkable feat, which undoubtedly should yield equally remarkable progress.

Now there is a track record on which to base performance assessment. Nigerians also now have a firm basis for comparison. After eight years of legislative activity, one could now measure the progression of the legislative branch of Nigeria's evolving democratic government.

Membership of the National Assembly is through direct election; any citizen can seek election into the federal legislative houses, as long as he/she meets the age and educational requirements. For the Senate, the age requirement is thirty-five years, and the educational requirement is a school certificate. For the House of Representatives, the minimum age is thirty years, and the educational requirement is equivalent to that of the Senate. This educational requirement has been interpreted to mean first school leaving certificate.

The tenure of each of the two houses is four years, running concurrently. Members willing to retain their seat must seek reelection.

The tenure of the present legislators expires in 2015. The presiding officer of the Nigerian Senate is known as the Senate President, while that of the House of Representatives is the Speaker.

At joint sessions of the National Assembly, the Senate President presides, and in his absence the Speaker. Other principal officers of the Senate include the Deputy Senate President, the Chief Whip, the Senate Leader, and the leaders of the three political party's caucuses. These posts are replicated in the House of Representatives.

For efficient discharge of duties, the legislative houses operate a committee system. Members are appointed into several committees, based on personal interests and professional competence. The committees assist the legislature in performing its "oversight" function over various agencies of government.

In Nigeria, the constitutional responsibilities of the legislature include making laws for the peace, progress, and good governance of the country. The two houses also influence government policies through motions and resolutions. Some responsibilities are, however, exclusive to the Senate. These include the screening and confirmation of both members of the federal executive, (known as ministers), and ambassadorial nominees. On the account of these exclusive responsibilities, the Senate is regarded as the upper house of the National Assembly, and the House, the lower. The Senate President is the chairman of the National Assembly.

Both houses are constitutionally mandated to seat for at least 181 days in a year.

Nigeria's National Assembly is located in the "new" federal capital city, Abuja.

CHAPTER 2

Functions of the National Assembly

Introduction

emocracy is a vital instrument that propels political proficiency, economic development, and social stability of any nation state. This is easily actualized where there is a high level legislative efficiency and efficacy. The National Assembly of any country is a binding force that transforms the politics and governance of that state into a scenario that maximally addresses the yearnings and aspirations of the downtrodden. Democracy in Nigeria has been a mere political desideratum hanging on a limping utopia.

Simply put, in our country Nigeria, the National Assembly dictates the operational mechanism of democracy, with certain sharp contradictions arising from defined self interest, instead of democracy dictating the operations of National Assembly.

A true democracy is a sine qua non for the development of all sectors of any country's economy. Golden (2010, 82) conceptualizes democracy to incorporate the exploitative and allienative tendencies often demonstrated by the capitalists against the downtrodden. According to him, democracy, empirically speaking, could mean "a socioeconomic and political formation that grants the hoi polloi the irreducible instrument of determining and participating effectively in the day-to-day smooth governance of their country." That is, the general transformative and restructuring powers of that state are vested in the hands of the electorates.

The rudiments of a true democracy are good governance, fair and legitimate elections, justice, equity, accountability, transparency, responsible leadership, political education of the masses, efficient political institutions, and respect for the rule of law. This means that a democratic environment creates an atmosphere where elections are free and fair, where legislative seats held by parties are as a result of votes received from the most recent elections and not as a result of cross-carpeting and where, if there is no clear majority in the legislature, several parties may come together to form a coalition government. Hence, democracy is not inimical to any well-organized chosen form of government, but fascism, Nazism, despotism, corruptocracy, favoritism, nepotism, and prebendalism are some profound enemies of equality, liberty, fraternity, and true representation, which are the symbols of democracy proper (Jakande 2008, 85). One can then ask the question, "Is Nigeria anywhere close to any of the above?" And one can comfortably answer, "We are trying but corruption must give way for us to get it right." Again, democracy must give room for the multiparty system to thrive. The advocates of multiparty system to be represented in government and often provided stable, enduring systems of government as in most countries in Europe. The practice of the so-called democracy in the twenty-first century Nigeria is intrinsically characterized by political instability, social macabre, cultural balderdash, and economic quagmire, resulting in unemployment of all forms, leading to abject hunger and indescribable poverty. The attendant implication of this misnomer are practical existence of all manner of crimes such as kidnapping, armed robbery, prostitution, sexual slavery, pen robbery, and electioneering, bickering, and hooliganism.

Other problems according to Dike (2011, 34) are corruption, the inability of the political class to transcend politics, the ubiquitous military, and the vast array of other factors that have characterized the Nigerian polity since independence. On the other hand, favoritism, nepotism, and corruption have become the de facto norm in the society on the side of employment opportunities, with meritocracy tossed out of the window. As in the past, the current economic and political problem in the society explains the recent upsurge of crises in Nigeria.

Since 1980 to date, the excruciating economic conditions were made unbearable by the constant devaluation of the nation's currency as well as the pronounced reoccurring degenerating crises in the oil sector of the nation's economy. The ugly economic scenario in Nigeria has negatively affected the nation's population that about 75.98 percent live below the poverty level (Chikelue 2011, 38).

Simply put, the general success of any practicing democracy is deeply incumbent upon three major challenges. First, the challenge of legislative efficiency, in which the activities of the National Assembly ought to reflect and reform positively the socioeconomic and political lacuna that has evaded the country for some reasonable length of while. Second is the challenge of the executive and management of the nation's economy. Last, is the willingness of the legislative powers to grant much reverenced policy of inclusiveness to the hoi polloi to participate vibrantly in the daily governance of the country (Mamudu and Hassan 2011, 24). Driving from this tangible assertion, the legislature is the umbrella that sheds and determines the shape and survival of any country with the people therein. The book therefore raises some fundamental questions with respect to the above empirical issues: Has the National Assembly in Nigeria been able to transform the poor economic status of the citizenry since 2003 to date? Has Nigerian National Assembly really able to demonstrate some fundamental practices of real democracy? These questions, without any prejudice to contemporary scholarship, would afford us the necessary interpretative guide to actualize some radical analytical construct in this book *Nigeria: X-ray of Issues and the Way Forward*

The National Assembly, by the virtue of its organ, is expected to build national structure on the solid and permanent foundation of social justice to fight against prejudices, wrong notions, and outworn customs and traditions to preach the fundamental principles of rule of law, and make it the underlying philosophy of political and social institutions.

Nigeria, a state that faces with a lot of challenges, embedded with corruption, discrimination, favoritism, ethnicity, injustice, and the like, the National Assembly is expected to dig deep into these challenges, which crippled Nigerian as a state and make a good legislative approach that will better the life of its citizenry. This should be our hallmark for any legislative and political wrangling.

The National Assembly as It Is

The *National Assembly* of the *Federal Republic of Nigeria* is a *bicameral* legislature established under section 4 of the Nigerian Constitution. It consists of a 109-member *Senate* and a 360-member *House of Representatives*. The body, modeled after the federal *Congress* of the *United States*, is supposed to guarantee equal representation of the *states* irrespective of size in the Senate and *proportional representation* of population in the House. The Assembly has broad oversight functions and is empowered to establish committees of its members to scrutinize *bills* and the conduct of government officials. Since the restoration of *democratic rule* in 1999, the Assembly has been said to be a "learning process" that has witnessed the election and removal of several Presidents of the Senate, allegations of *corruption*, slow passage of private members' bills, and the creation of ineffective committees to satisfy numerous interests.

The Senate has the unique power of impeachment of *judges* and other high officials of the executive including the federal *Auditor-General* and the members of the electoral and revenue commissions. This power is, however, subject to prior request by the president. The Senate also confirms the president's nomination of senior *diplomats*, members of the federal *cabinet*, federal *judicial* appointments, and independent federal commissions.

Before any bill may become law, it must be agreed to by both the House and the Senate, and receive the president's assent. Should the president delay or refuse assent (*veto*) the bill, the Assembly may pass the law by two-thirds of both chambers and overrule the veto, and the president's consent will not be required.

Basis for Its Existence and Why We Should Be Informed

The major distinguishing feature of democracy that sets it apart from other systems of governance is the presence of a legislature. It is not merely a form of decoration for the system, which colonial authorities had in Nigeria. The legislature, in a democracy, exists as an independent institution with its unique life and process, which deepen democracy and ultimately strengthen the polity. It arose from deep dissatisfaction with monarchy, a one-man rule in which the king presumes to be God or answers to God only.

The legislature emerged as a result of the need for people to run their affairs. It arose from the need to make government accountable to the people. This need for accountability has ensured that all activities of parliament are open to public scrutiny. Parliamentary processes have evolved around openness and accountability. Parliamentary processes actually open up all governmental affairs for public scrutiny. The legislature as the representative of the people is also expected to follow up its legislations to make sure that they are obeyed or are flawless, hence the oversight function, which gives the legislature the needed information to amend or strengthen or even abolish laws.

The inability of the elected assemblies to check the performance of the executive arm of the state has led to dismay and increasing disillusion by Nigerians about the real value of democracy. State governments sack local government chairmen. The president privatizes the nation, and no one knows exactly how, where, or who pays for what. Nothing is accounted for. One could then ask, "Are we practicing true democracy as it ought to be practiced?" The answer by most people will be a big fat no. We need to strengthen our democracy.

The National Assembly as matter of urgency should inform the public on how the affairs of government are run and also make sure that yearly budgets are implemented to the later. An independent legislature that is comprised of elected members representing various constituents should be a true test of freedom in our democracy but is it a true picture of what are experiencing? The answer again is simply no. A country or a nation without a free and independent parliament cannot experience true freedom. We must act now and act fast. The people must govern not a selected few. The House of Representative gives the masses their say in the counsels of power. Public policy issues need for good representative solutions on the approach of consensus building needs the many view points of the people through their representations. In any legitimate government, it is an established fact that the people ought to be sovereign that means the sole authority of governance rest with the people. This assertion in itself defines democracy as government of the people by the people and for the people. Under this guideline no elected official is supreme, in other words they are branded "servant rulers." John Adams (American founders constitution, chap. 4, document 5) wrote, "A representative assembly", should be in miniature, an exact portrait of the people been represented. It should think, feel, reason, and act like them. As well as been accountable to them and that is the beauty of a democracy that works." (Adams 1776)

What Core Principles Guide Its Existence?

Every society is governed by laws, and lawmaking is a higher calling. In democratic setting like Nigeria, the legislature emerged to make law to govern the country. The core principles are the philosophy that guides the legislative management styles, policies, strategies, and operational performance. The National Assembly should work toward inevitability of the legislature's policy making, representational, and oversight functions in tackling major challenges facing democratic transition in Nigeria. The National Assembly is an official body, usually chosen by election not selection, with the power to make, change, and repeal laws, as well as powers to represent the constituent units and control government. "A powerful legislature is needed to engender a democracy in which people have some real decision making power over and above the formal consent of electoral choice." In their own analysis, Johnson and Nakamura pointed out that "effective legislatures contribute to effective governance by performing important functions necessary to sustain democracy in complex and diverse societies." To them, "democratic societies need the arena for the airing of societal differences provided by representative assemblies with vital ties to the populace." They need institutions that are capable of writing good laws in both the political sense of getting agreement from participants and in the technical sense of achieving the intended purposes. The legislature should be guided by the core principle of their existence to sustain the democracy. Good representative institutions are expected to connect their constituents to their government "by giving them a place where their needs can be articulated, by giving them a say in shaping the rules that govern them, by providing them with recourse if governmental power is abused, and by contributing to the procedures and values that sustain a democratic culture." In the parliamentary system, the legislature is considered as the soul of government, since the executive derives its power and legitimacy from parliament.

In a democracy, legislatures play three major roles: they express the will of the people, they pass laws, and they hold government, particularly the executive, to account. They also control and administer national budgets. Put differently, legislative institutions perform rule making, representational, and oversight functions, which have serious implications for national development.

What Are the Relations between the National Assembly and the Presidency?

The emerging conclusions from studies on democratic governance all over the world as well as experience from all other places with regard to the practice of democracy show that it is replete with serious problems everywhere and as we all know it. It is individually observed aptly that "democracy is the most widely admired type of political system but also the most difficult to sustain." With regard to Africa, mostly Nigeria, two of the most daunting challenges facing the continent today revolve around the institutionalization of democratic governance and the achievement of sustainable human development. The relationship between the National Assembly and presidency should be cordial for the smooth running of the country. In Nigeria there are wide speculations that the National Assembly is a rubber stamp to the executive, that they do not carry out their oversight function as enshrined in the constitution of the Federal Republic of Nigeria. They find it difficult to checkmate the excessiveness of the presidency, and that is the reason the office of the presidency seems as the most powerful in the land.

The recent summon by the National Assembly to the president to explain why provisions of yearly budget as was passed by the National Assembly could not be implemented is a clear indication that the legislature is realizing their oversight function as the chief custodian of law of the land; because to exercise its oversight function, a reserve power permits them under sections 88 and 89 to summon "any person, authority, ministry, or government department charged with the authority of executing laws and disbursing or administering money appropriated or to be appropriated by the National Assembly." But to the contrary, the president is not obligated to stand before the National Assembly or is forbidden by law from the Hallowed Chambers of the National Assembly except on occasion/s permitted by his function, such as his annual address to the joint sitting of the National Assembly on the State of the Nation Address, or the presentation of his budget, or in the company of a visiting head of government granted the courtesy of addressing the joint sitting of Nigeria's National Assembly—or in the extreme— upon his impeachment. Then the question is, "The president, is he above the law?" It seems the framers of Nigerian constitution, in creating the buffer that prohibits the Assembly from simply summoning the president, did so to protect the office from whimsical, mischievous, and derogative action and errant legislation. The president is not above the law and cannot be held above the law when it comes to his personal and official conduct. Therefore, he is not the most powerful office in the land. The National Assembly should see themselves as the most powerful office in the land and should start judiciously as a matter of urgency to scrutinize the function of government, and to prevent the excesses or even failures of executive power. They should know why the federal and state yearly budgets are hardly implemented. Every year, Nigerians are presented with government expenditures that do not reflect either in their quality of life or in the improvement of social services. It is the oversight function of the legislature to form a credible monitoring process to match what is on paper to what is on ground. Since the inception of the fourth republic, the working relationship between the National Assembly and the presidency seems to be cordial with multiplicity of corruptions all over the nation. The house hardly carryout their oversight functions as established by law to scrutinize the excesses of the presidency. The inability of the elected assemblies to check the performance of the executive arm of the state has made the presidency to be in slumber in carrying out their executive role.

What Are the Strongholds of the National Assembly?

The lawmaking function is one of the essential pillars of any society. No human society survives in the total absence of laws. Whatever the social system, the conduct of affairs must be defined by certain basic rules. These rules must be made by someone or some group and executed or enforced by some group. In a democratic environment, power belongs to the people who in turn elect those who are to carry out the task of lawmaking on their behalf but in a despot and directly exercised by him or assigned to anyone of his choice. There are no clear lines demarcating the lawmaking function from the executive function. The two flows into each other and are often carried out by the same people. Therefore, the story of one inevitably leads to the other. Such is the case of law-making in Nigeria, arising from its long history of military dictatorships. The story of the legislature is intertwined with that of the executive and evolves from the larger history of the Nigerian national itself. Nothing better captures this evolution than the process of constitutional engineering in Nigeria, for it is these supreme laws of the land that provide guidance for lawmaking.

The National Assembly suited in Abuja derives its strength to make law that governs the land through its oversight function by the sovereignty of the people of Nigerians who elected them.

The behavior of members of the National Assembly sometimes suggests that Nigerians are yet to imbibe civilized values in the art and science of lawmaking. The general impression is that if the National Assembly can be bribed to mutilate the constitution, then what is the merit of its stronghold as the chief custodian of law. Since democracy is majority rule, majority of the National Assembly members can be patronized to turn the constitution upside down. The attitude of lawmakers in matters concerning state interest is far below the expectation of the Nigerian masses. Taking the oath to make laws is more like a spiritual testament to serve the people because the soul of a nation is inextricably linked to the soul of a nation. The National Assembly should understand that "Sovereignty belongs to the people of Nigeria from whom government through its Constitution derives all its powers and authority."

The people of Nigerian have mandated the legislature to work toward the development of Nigerians by passing positive law that will reduce the suffering of the citizenry. They should work to maintain the very existence of the country as a single political entity, so as to ensure its survival and preserve its unity; they have to make radical changes in the system.

Individual Liberties and the National Assembly

The supreme laws or constitutions are products of the dynamic polity; it is a part of the political history of Nigeria. The development of the legislature can be achieved on how the National Assembly comport themselves in the act of lawmaking. The legislature is not an extension of the executive but a coordinate and complementary branch of the government, which derives its legitimacy and authority from the Constitution. It is therefore equally responsible for the governance of the nation as the executive. It has an independent existence, with independent powers, functions, or duties and should therefore not be seen as a mere rubber stamp of the executive policies and decisions. The National Assembly should work to develop men with the necessary technological training to supply the needs of modern industry and agriculture. There is great need for them to develop men who may assume positions of responsibility in the management of business and industry. In order to effect an orderly and scientific development of the economy and to permit the intelligent planning of the production sector of the general economy, it is essential for them as soon as possible to undertake a survey of the economy of Nigerian by making positive law that will improve the economy through the act of lawmaking. The individual liberties of the legislature should be respected in all ramifications but must be in line with the core principles, code of conduct that established the National Assembly. The National Assembly must work hard to give to all matters concerning the future security of the country, the earnest consideration their fundamental importance deserves. If eternal vigilance is the price of freedom, let them then be ceaselessly vigilant. Nigerian defensive system requires no unusual sacrifice by any individual, but its success depends primarily and almost exclusively upon a unification of the efforts of all toward the common and vital purpose. To attain such unification in a democracy, the military plan must be supported by popular intelligence, confidence, and enthusiasm. It is a special function of government to see that confidence is fairly earned and assiduously sustained. The legislature should see that every law they pass and every military measure they adopt shall reflect an unselfish and national purpose, that it shall impose injustice on none, and that it shall promote the security and defend the peace, the possessions, and the liberty of Nigerians. The individual liberties of the National Assembly should be a self-sacrifice for the nation's interest.

How Successful Has the National Assembly Been?

The National Assembly occupies a prominent and pivotal position as the apex lawmaking organ of government under the 1999 Constitution.

A strong legislature is vital to a democratic system of government. A democratic government is based on a system of limited constitutional authority distributed to different decision structures. This ensures that major political decisions are taken after thorough deliberations. The ultimate goal of creating multiple power centers is to ensure that they checkmate each other and thereby prevent the emergence of a dictator. The intricate interrelationships between the multiple power centers and the mechanisms for ensuring that they work are the ingredients of constitutionalism. In this scheme of power sharing, the legislature plays a more enhanced role in a presidential democracy than in a parliamentary democracy. The legislature is still regarded by many too immature in the process of lawmaking, as a result of their failure to abide by the principle of their oversight functions.

Looking back in time, in 1999, the first symptom of legislative high-handedness at the National Assembly was manifested in the demand for the outrageous "Furniture Allowance." The legislators displayed affluence without regard to the prevailing poverty in the land. The furniture allowance debate was their most profound achievement in their first one hundred days in the office. In Nigeria, there are many knotty issues to address as a nation. The level of insecurity is frightening. The monster of insecurity of lives and property metaphorically walks the streets of major towns and cities. Most of our roads are shorthand for death traps, while the educational system is in dire jeopardy, as standards are fast fading with no one to the rescue. There is need to reposition of Nigerian Police Force; the electoral reforms have not made a headway. There is real work to be done. There are power sector reforms, which have been on the front burners. Why are National Assembly members active only when it comes to matters affecting their welfare such as upward review of their allowances? This is the question ask by many Nigerian who perceive the lawmakers as people working for their own interest instead of Nigerian interest. Since 1999, the National Assembly is enmeshed with one kind of corruption to the other that leads to the impeachment of many Senate President and Speakers. There are many cases of gross misconduct at the Hallowed Chamber. For instance the Speaker of the House of Representatives, Dimeji Bankole, was alleged to be at the center of the N5.2 billion Rural Electrification Agency scam; the chairman of Senate Committee on Power, Nicholas Ugbane, and his House of Representatives counterpart, Ndudi Elumelu, were also indicted.

As the chief custodian, in spite of the negative principles associated with the legislature, they have played a major role in stabilizing the polity. The National Assembly saves the country from the crisis that would have emanated as a result of President Yar'adua's ill health by invoking the doctrine of necessity. The have passed many bills that will improve the living condition of the citizenry, but they failed to checkmate in ensuring that the executive arm implement it to the later.

CHAPTER 3

The Effect of the National Assembly

Our Welfare and the National Assembly

The legislators make laws and appropriate funds for various national projects. The welfare of the citizenry must be the most priority of every legislator. Sovereignty of the people elected them to make law that will guarantee good governance to assure the welfare of the citizenry. Some of the legislators put the welfare of Nigerians behind and pursue their own welfare. This is the reason Owelle Anayo Rochas Okorocha put it in this direction, "That politicians think of the next election while leaders think of the next generation." Our legislators do not think the welfare of the people but rather to package their welfare for the next election. The National Assembly should always stand by the tenets of good governance and true representation at all times.

Democratic practices and good governance flourish in an environment where political elites possess the required leadership skills and know-how anchored on the tenets of democracy. It is essential that they represent a broader constituency beyond their immediate surroundings in articulating their respective policies, which derive from a sound knowledge of the rudiments of interest aggregation.

The legislators should cultivate the spirit of visionary, courageous, selfless leadership, and the will to restore the country to socioeconomic, political, and moral health. Each member of the National Assembly is expected by the citizenry who voted them in to be a quintessential statesman or stateswoman who has the welfare of the people at heart and work to make law that will alleviate the deplorable living standard of the people.

The perception of the masses is that our elected men and women in the Hallow Chamber have deserted us and that they don't think about the sovereignty of the citizens who elected them). There is insecurity in the land, our roads are death traps, no good drinking water, and no electricity, yet every year budget is passed with trillions of naira, but no one cares to ask how the sovereignty of people are.

This is the reason Femi Falana stated in Channel Television that "Crude oil per production per day = 2.5m barrels. Current price is $113 per barrel, Daily sales = 2.5m × $113 = $282.5 million. Monthly sales = $282.5m × 30 days = $8.475 billion. Yearly sales = $8.475 billion × 12 = $101.7 billion. Naira Equivalent = 101.7 billion × N160 = N16.272 trillion. Nigerian budget for the 2012 = N 4.5 trillion. The surplus is 16.272 trillion - 4.5 trillion = 11.712." Now the question is where the surplus of 11.712 trillion is going?

Falana's explanation concludes what former US President Bill Clinton said that Nigeria is too rich to be poor.

The National Assembly do not play progressive role in National development, and this could be deduced from their overt reluctance or out-right failure to checkmate the executive arm on the implementation of the nation's yearly budget. The National Assembly should imbibe the spirit of good governance so that by their political education, convictions, and inclinations, they are a democracy. They have to establish a democratic system of government, and the perpetuation of this system will depend upon their ability to convince the people that democracy can be freed from those vices, which have destroyed some countries, and that it can be made as efficient as any other system of government known to man. The legislatures have to prove the sovereignty of people that through a wise use of democratic processes, the welfare and the safety of the people can be promoted, thus contributing our share to the preservation of democracy in the world.

What Role Does Government Play?

Constitution under section 13 stipulates that it shall be the duty and responsibility of all organs of government, and of all authorities and persons, exercising legislative, executive, or judicial powers, to conform to, observe, and apply the provisions of the Constitution on the fundamental objectives and directive principles of state policy as contained in chapter 2 of the Constitution of the Federal Republic of Nigeria. This means that government is required by the supreme law of the land (the constitution) to see to it that provisions on the fundamental objectives and directive principles of state policy are implemented to the letter. The question is, "Did government carry its functions as enshrined in the Constitution?" If government is to play its role for good governance, government should abide by the principles of this objective of the Constitution under section 13.

Government should understand that Nigerians have invested power on them to legislate and implement laws passed by its legislative arms through different ministries and departments, agencies, assistance of career civil, and public servants; to formulate the general policies of government; to sign international agreements or treaties between Nigeria and other countries; to coordinate the activities of various ministries and parastatals by supervising their performance and functions; to ensure maintenance of law and order through its various security agencies; and to prepare the annual budget for good governance, transparency, accountability, and equity for the good of all. Government should work hard to raise the standard of the legislative arm to people's expectations to ensure that it is corruption free. Most often, the National Assembly has been enmeshed with many profound scandals from one administration to the other: from Chuba Okadigbo to Adolphus Nwagbara, from Speaker of the House;

Patricia Eteh to Dimeji Bankole, etc. In a separate incident, a bribery scandal in the Federal Ministry of Education led some senators to tender their resignation as either committee chairmen or members on the floor of the Senate. There were allegations of the MTN bribery. Prior to the alleged scam, MTN gave N4.4 million worth of free recharge cards to members of the National Assembly; in view of all this, government is expected to play a role to give enhanced support for greater democracy, effective governance and transparency, and to help fight corruption and return stolen assets.

The National Assembly and Nigeria as It Is Today

Our constitution vests the presidency and the National Assembly with powers to direct the affairs of the nation. The legislators make laws and appropriate funds for various national projects, while the president signs the laws and sees to the execution of the projects in line with the appropriated funds. It is supposed to be a system of checks and balances in which the presidency prepares the budget, often in collaboration with the National Assembly, while the legislators approve or disapprove. Then it goes back to the presidency for implementation. The National Assembly is expected to be an institution free from corruption to enable to make laws that will govern the nation without fear or favor. As it may, the National Assembly has been slow in making laws that will move Nigeria forward. Since 1999, when the National Assembly assume full power to make law without interruption from the military, they have not been able to carry their day to day activities in terms of lawmaking well. Nigerian have seen a lot of loop holes from the side of the National Assembly that make citizenry begin to ask if they are honorable men as they claim to be. What we have been getting from our elected men in the house is impeachment upon impeachment base on corrupt practices from the lower house to the upper house. On the electoral reform, which is the stronghold of good democracy, the National Assembly have not done much in that area. The citizenry expected the National Assembly to update guidelines on the conduct of elections every year, but to them, it is not subject for discussion.

If the common defining property of democracy is that it is an electoral contest and context in which political parties compete for the votes of citizens at regular intervals, therefore for the election to be able to produce a legitimate government, citizens must be able to participate in the system both as voters and candidates for offices without fear otherwise anything outside this means the whole system has been programmed to fail.

Other area citizens complain about the National Assembly is the ongoing drama between them and the presidency. To Nigerian scholars, why the National Assembly is fighting the presidency is as follows: that the conflicts are between two corrupt and inefficient institutions that have lose their integrity. What is clear is that corruption and inefficiency are at the roots of the ongoing conflict between the two. An interesting dimension of the conflict is the threat of impeachment by the House of Representatives, based, as it were, on the president's slow pace of budget implementation and his failure to implement it as appropriated. It is a familiar tactic that the National Assembly has employed against all presidents since 1999. There are two scripts about the sources of the ongoing conflict. The official script highlights two factors, namely the president's poor implementation of the 2012 budget and the lethargy with which he has been treating the bills and resolutions passed by the National Assembly.

Specifically, the House of Representatives accuses the president of treating the 2012 budget with so much levity that only about 35 percent implementation had been achieved as of the end of July, leaving only about five months to go to the end of the year when ministries, departments, and agencies would be required to return unspent budget funds to the treasury. As for the president's slow pace in treating bills and resolutions, the House is particularly concerned about Jonathan's lackadaisical treatment of the report of the fuel subsidy probe and his refusal to honor the House's resolution for him to explain his plans to curb escalating insecurity.

On the surface, these are genuine complaints. The question, however, is, "How far is it true that the House is dissatisfied with the president in the public interest, as its leaders claim?" Is the House fighting for you and me or for its members' benefits? The answer lies in the motivation for their complaints, especially about budget implementation. And this is where the hidden script comes in.

It is a two-part hidden script. On the one hand, the National Assembly is concerned about the ripple effects of slow budget implementation on its members' wallets. When budget implementation is slow, the release of funds will be slow, and MDAs will not get funds for the projects earmarked in their budgets. Legislators are especially interested in the MDAs' budgets because they are known to inflate the budgets of various MDAs and negotiate their share of the pork once funds are released to them.

Legislators are particularly interested in constituency projects, which American politicians call "pork." They are padded on appropriation bills by legislators as projects dear to their constituencies. When funds for capital projects are not released, there would be no funds for constituency projects. You can now understand that the legislators' complaint about the slow release of funds to the MDAs is not completely altruistic, Nigerian scholars say.

The National Assembly has contributed in small measure to the growth of democracy in Nigerian, which we believe at the learning process. Some bills they passed and amended, if well implemented will change the fortune of Nigerian citizens. But they have not work hard to make sure that the bills the pass are implemented to the later, rather will influenced by the presidency and that ends the matter. The National Assembly through its exercise of investigative powers and establishment of some legal instruments was able to expose some corrupt practices between 1999 and 2008.

The National Assembly are not worried about the risen poverty in the country what they are after is their pocket. Most often when they initiate to eradication corruption, the dragon that cage the growth of the nation by opting for probe on various sectors of the economy, what next, they dangle into corruption that will lead to the close of the matter. Nigerian citizens have not fed well at this democratic era, rather they are subjected to various hard economic policies from different governments that endanger the livelihood of the common man, and moreover those policies will never be implemented. Insecurity is on the high rise, infrastructural facilities have been decayed, our educational systems hit the rock without anyone to rescue it, yet we have the National Assembly in the making.

The Burden on the National Assembly

The National Assembly occupies a prominent and pivotal position as the apex lawmaking organ of government under the 1999 Constitution.

According to *Peter A. Akhihiero ESQ*, a strong legislature is vital to a democratic system of government. A democratic government is based on a system of limited constitutional authority distributed to different decision structures. This ensures that major political decisions are taken after thorough deliberations. The ultimate goal of creating multiple power centers is to ensure that they checkmate each other and thereby prevent the emergence of a dictator.

The intricate interrelationships between the multiple power centers and the mechanisms for ensuring that they work are the ingredients of constitutionalism.

Apart from that, the National Assembly is saddled with numerous burdens that affect them as institutions. First, how to get the capacity of legislatures, federal, state, and local that could be strengthened to address critical issues relating to constitutionalism, corruption, poverty, and national question, check the excesses of the executive, and collaborate with the judiciary to avert the consequences of "democracy by court order," as well as empower and work with the civil society. Second, how to get a more proactive National Assembly that is ready to set the priorities right as well as resolve its internal crisis democratically.

How Do We See the National Assembly?

Loewenberg conceptualizes legislatures as "assemblies of elected representatives from geographically defined constituencies, with lawmaking functions in the governmental process." In the same vein, Jewell identified two features that distinguish legislatures from other branches of government. According to him, "They (legislatures) have formal authority to pass laws, which are implemented and interpreted by the executive and judicial branches, and their members normally are elected to represent various elements in the population."

According to Roberts and Edwards, "Popular participation, absolute respect for the rule of law, a general guarantee of fundamental freedoms which lubricate popular participation, periodic, competitive, free and fair elections with the vote of every citizen counting equally, respect for majority rule as well as the readiness of minority to acquiesce in the decision of the majority, accountability, guarantee of separation of powers in practice, transparency, and responsiveness in governance and opportunity for change of government or any leadership found wanting."

To Nigerians, the National Assembly is not meeting the expectations of the citizenry. For instance, the 1999 Constitution of the Federal Republic of Nigeria empowers the assemblies both federal and state to perform the following functions among others:

    a. Lawmaking and policy formulation functions

  b. Oversight functions
  c. Investigative functions

d. The role of the watchdog of public funds, derived from the legislatures powers and duties with regard to public finance

e. Representative or constituency responsibilities role

Despite the powers, functions, and privileges provided for the legislature in most Nigerian constitutions after independence, comments, and observations have shown that this organ has not lived up to expectation. The Report of Political Bureau in 1987 is more revealing. According to the report, "It is a well known fact that up until 1979, legislatures were the weakest link in the making of public policies in Nigeria. Between the establishment of the Nigerian Council by Lugard soon after the amalgamation of the Southern and Northern Protectorates of Nigeria in 1914 and the end of the first thirteen years of military rule, public policy making was dominated by the executive. Indeed, a national daily newspaper in 1963 referred to the Federal Legislature as an 'expensive and irrelevant talking shop.'"

The second and aborted third republic's legislatures did not improve significantly in terms of their performance. Even from recent analyses, the new democratic dispensation ushered in on May 29, 1999, has not significantly changed the situation. Ibeanu and Egwu, while analyzing the eight years of democratic rule in Nigeria, vividly demonstrated that "basic institutions of democratic governance especially the legislature and the judiciary remain weak and vulnerable to executive manipulation under conditions of enormous concentration of power and resources in the executive presidency."

So many reasons have been adduced for the declining role of the legislature, particularly at the center, in Nigeria—long periods of military rule; absence of well-established political parties and political process; personal ambition, interest, and agenda of legislators; dysfunctional constituents; corruption; adverse legislative environment; as well as the presence of amateur legislators in great number, and the shortage of staff aides (due to the lack of continuity in legislative membership), as well as executive-legislative squabbles account for the poor performance of the National Assembly and state legislatures in the discharge of its function. Even at the level of the legislature, multiparty politics has actually led to a reduction in politics. In other words, the ruling party dominates its members as well as the nation, in the name of party discipline, while the so-called opposition strives to take their place, without challenging the basic structure or content of political rule and economic framework as well as resolve its internal crisis democratically.

How Do We Evaluate Members of the National Assembly?

The restoration of constitutional rule in May 1999 heralded the new democratic order in which the numerous challenges of democratic governance and development facing Nigeria were expected to be effectively addressed. The National Assembly is expected to build political will, which is needed to combat political corruption, legislative system must foster personal integrity of legislators through codes of conduct for legislators—disclosure of assets, conflict of interest, enacting legislation on campaign, and political party finance; building transparency in wage levels and benefits; ensuring that legislative immunity is not abused; enacting legislation regarding the freedom of information; and protecting whistleblowers. It is important to bring about system adjustment in countries where these supporting mechanisms are absent. This may involve counterbalancing the power between the legislature and executive and, in some cases, between the state and civil society.

Most often, corruption is confronted frontally with several programs initiated and institutions established and approved by the National Assembly to ensure accountability, probity, and transparency in governance. Between 2000 and 2001, the Budget Office was created out of the Ministry of Finance and the Budget Monitoring Unit and Price Intelligence Unit (BMPIU) popularly referred to as the Due Process Unit. The raison d'être was to bring sanity and prudence into public expenditure, budgeting, and public procurement in Nigeria, which before now were lucrative avenues for corrupt public officials to loot the treasury. To get public officers involved in the anti-corruption crusade, the presidency approved the recommendation that anti-corruption and transparency monitoring units in all government departments. The National Assembly, in compliance with the directive from the then Head of Service of the Federation vide a circular referenced OHCSF/ MS/192/94, dated October 2, 2001, accepted an Anti-Corruption and Transparency Monitoring Unit (ACTU) operating within its sphere of activity. In addition, the federal executive with the approval of the National Assembly created the Extractive Industries Transparency Initiative (ETTI) aimed at monitoring the extractive industry to know exactly what is being extracted and the revenue accruing there from. This step has encouraged transparency and accountability in the extractive industries as resources extracted and revenue paid by the companies are received by government and the sum NEPA Fund, that could not be properly accounted for by the then National Electric Power Authority (NEPA) Officials. Similarly, the former Minister of Aviation, Dr. (Mrs.) Kema Chikwe, and the director-general of the Bureau for Public Enterprise (BPE) were summoned to appear before the committee of the National Assembly on the privatization of the Nigerian Airways Limited (NAL), and the establishment of a new national airline. The secret deals of the ministry were exposed, and the plans to purchase the assets of NAL under shrouded circumstances were scuttled. Although there have been accusations against members of the legislative committees for using this avenue to procure contracts from these administrative bodies, however, the power of investigation was employed by the National Assembly to summon most of the ministers and the personnel of their ministries to appear before it to furnish them with explanations on certain major governmental policies and activities.

CHAPTER 4

How the National Assembly Works

What Type of Institution Is It?

The National Assembly is an institution vested with power to make law that governs the land. This is done through code and norms together with the principles of collective responsibility among the elected members. Responsibilities of the legislature include making laws for the peace, progress, and good governance of the country. The two houses also influence government policies through motions and resolutions (Okosun 2005, 19). Some responsibilities are, however, exclusive to the Senate. These include the screening and confirmation of both members of the federal executive (known as ministers) and ambassadorial nominees.

On the account of these exclusive responsibilities, the Senate is regarded as the upper house of the National Assembly, and the House, the lower. The Senate President is the chairman of the National Assembly.

The legislature was one of the causalities of Nigeria's first military rule, which spanned from January 17, 1966, to October 1, 1976. During this period, most democratic structures, prominent among was the legislature were abolished, while the military rulers operated a unitary system of government. The second republic was ushered in on October 1, 1979, through a groundwork prepared by the constitution drafting committee and a constituent assembly.

According to Olugbenga (2008, 20), these two bodies functioned between 1978 and 1979 and produced the Constitution of the Federal Republic of Nigeria 1979. This Constitution provided for an executive presidential system of government, whose features include separation of powers among the three arms of government, viz. the executive, legislature, and judiciary. The second republic legislature was also bicameral. There was a Senate, with a membership strength of ninety-five (each of them nineteen states in the country produced five senators) and a Federal House of Representatives with a membership strength of 450. The second republic was abruptly terminated by a military coup on December 31, 1983.

The third republic took off via a transition programmed mid-wife in 1985 by the military president Ibrahim Babangida administration. The imposed transition program resulted in the election of ninety-one senators to the National Assembly in December 1992, with each of the then thirty states producing three senators, and the Federal Capital Territory producing a seat. The Federal House of Representatives, however, had membership strength of 593; the seats were filled on the basis of one representative per each of the 593 local governments existing then in the country.

The annulment of the June 12, 1993, presidential election and the resulting political crisis thereof, led to the overthrow of the pseudo democratic government led then by Chief Ernest Shonekan on November 17, 1993. Nigeria did not witness democracy again until May 29, 1999, when the General Abdulsalam Abubakar military junta handed over to a democratically elected government under the leadership of President Olusegun Obasanjo.

This fourth republic was anchored on the 1999 Constitution, whose features are not substantially different from the 1979 Constitution. It provides for a bicameral legislature—the Senate and the Federal House of Representatives. The former is composed of 109 members, three each from the thirty-six states in the country; while the latter is composed of 360 members representing federal constituencies on an almost equal population basis. However, since the restoration of democratic rule in 1999, the Assembly has been said to be a "learning process" that has witnessed the election and removal of several presidents of the Senate, allegations of corruption, slow passage of private member's bills, and the creation of ineffective committees to satisfy numerous interests (Olumide 2010, 23). For instance, between 2003 and February 2011, several bills have been passed into law by the assembly but without any radical approach to salvage the economic yearnings and aspirations of the down trodden. All these bills were not only bills that would attract more contracts to enrich the already rich pockets of the house members but also very insensitive in moving the socioeconomic and political base of the country to the next level. Unemployment was the order of the day, as hunger, abject poverty, and high-level crimes have taken the stage (Akindele 2011, 26).

National Assembly is expected to be an institution that will be the mirror of the sovereignty of the people, free from corruption in a bid to make and pass laws that will salvage the economic yearning and aspiration of the citizens and ensure that those bills passed are implemented to the latter.

A Member of the National Assembly Wears Many Hats

The National Assembly should be a body of people marked off by common descent, language, culture, or historical tradition. As a body elected by various constituencies, it is expected to be goal-oriented people toward the development of the nationhood. Discipline toward national interest should be the chief objective of every members of the National Assembly. They should know why they are elected and what those who elected them expect from each member. They should demonstrate their abiding love for our nation to the end that they may emerge to play its proper role in the uplifting of the African Continent and the socio economic development of the people. The National Assembly should work to create several small states of corresponding ethnic differences. The legislature as a body that wears many hats should know that although the problem of devising a workable and lasting system of government for Nigeria is far from easy, nevertheless, they must not lose hope or abandon the aspirations and expectations that have been held for so long. They shall return to the theme of searching for political stability after saying a few words on the position of the people of Nigeria under the Constitution in the system of government. The National Assembly should understand that Nigeria cannot hope to survive as a nation unless it is able to produce leaders of the right quality and caliber to guide its affairs. In making law or amending the existing law, they should know that a Constitution, which fails to throw up the right type of leaders from time to time, may well be regarded as inadequate for one of the most vital of the objectives designed to achieve. On the other hand, as a body of people that wears many hats, should bear in mind that the Constitution does not make the leaders. It merely lays down the rules for their selection and the regulation of their conduct and activities as trustees of power within the state. The democratic system ensures that the selection shall be made by the people themselves or by their accredited representatives (lawmakers), and in this sense, the ultimate responsibility for ensuring quality rests with the people.

Constituency Representation: How? And What?

The National Assembly is an official body, usually chosen by election, with the power to make, change, and repeal laws, as well as powers to represent the constituent units and control government. Constituency representation is one of the major factors that make the National Assembly inactive. Most of our lawmakers do not know why they are elected to the National Assembly. Poor representation has denied the electorate of various constituencies the impact of democracy. ***Blackwell Encyclopedia of Political Science*** defines legislatures as political institutions whose members are formally equal to one another, whose authority derives from a claim that the members are representative of the political community, and whose decisions are collectively made according to complex procedures. Some lawmakers who represent various constituencies do know how those they are representing are feeling. They do not go to their constituency to find out the political need of their people. Most of them live in hotels throughout their tenure. If they do not come home, how would they know the needs of those who elected them? They will come home whenever there is an election to promise people heaven and earth, which they will not fulfill. Lawmakers should understand that good constituency representation is the success of a good democracy because they are the mouth-piece of the people.

How Does a Bill Become Law?

The lawmaking function is one of the essential pillars of any society. No human society survives in the total absence of laws. Whatever the social system, the conduct of affairs must be defined by certain basic rules. These rules must be made by someone or some group and executed or enforced by some group. In a democratic environment, power belongs to the people who in turn elect those who are to carry out the task of lawmaking on their behalf. For a bill to become law, it must undergo the following processes:

1. Introduction of a Bill – Each bill is assigned a number, read by title only and sponsor.

•   Private Bill - Any person or organization within Nigeria may initiate a law. This may only be presented to the

House or Senate through members of the National Assembly in his or her own name. Only a member of the National Assembly can introduce legislation on the floor of the House or Senate. Legislators, however, often introduce bills suggested by other individuals or organizations. Bills vary in length from a single paragraph to hundreds of pages.

- Executive Bill - This is initiated by or from the president of the Federal Republic or any department or agency of the Federal Government. It must, however, bear the signature of the president and is usually submitted to both chambers of the National Assembly.

2. Committee Consideration - Committee meetings are open to the public. (This is often not the case in Nigeria but should be the practice except when for overriding public reasons certain information ought not to be made public). A bill may be reported out of committee with one of the following reports: favorable, with amendments, favorable with committee substitutes, unfavorable, or without opinion. As a matter of fact, a committee may change completely the contents of a bill before reporting it out. A committee can essentially kill a bill by failing to act on it. Committees may summon any persons to appear before it. Committees may propose public hearings to the House. Under the House rules of the period 1999–2003, only a full session of the House can authorize public hearing.
3. Second Reading – The bill is read by title a second time and sent to the appropriate committee.

4. Third Reading and Passage - This motion is made by the house leader and initiates floor debate on a bill. Following debate and amendments, a final vote on the bill is taken. To pass, a bill must be approved by a majority of the members present and voting. If a bill is defeated, that is the end of it. If a bill passed in one chamber, it is sent to the other chamber where it follows the same procedure. Both chambers must agree on the final form of each bill. If either house fails to concur in amendments made by the other, a conference committee of senators and representatives must reconcile the difference. Compromises agreed to by conference committees are then subject to approval by both houses.

5. President Action - The president may sign a bill, permit it to become law without signing it, or veto it. The veto may be overridden by a two thirds majority of the members of the two houses. The president has thirty days to act on a bill after it has been received. After thirty days, the house leader may present the bill back to the National Assembly.

• Resolutions - Besides bills, the legislature may express its feelings in simple, concurrent, or joint resolutions. Simple resolutions require action by only one house. They are used to handle procedure, organization, or to express the sense of the chamber on a particular matter. Frequently, the House or Senate pass a simple resolution to adjourn in honor or memory of an individual.

Why Should We Be Well Informed before Electing Members?

The process of electing representatives of the people (electorate) into public offices is one that has become all the more challenging in many states of the world, especially in the developing countries like Nigeria. Lack of awareness among the electorate who chose members of the National Assembly to make laws that will advance the value of democracy is a fundamental factor that hinders the progress of democracy.

The progress of democracy is when the electorate is well informed about democracy, to know its fruits, why we need democracy, and how to choose those who will move democracy forward. Every citizens of democracy should be enlightened to choose credible people that will bring the fruits of democracy down to his constituency. Democracy is based on the notion that a people should be self-governing and that the representatives of the people should be held accountable for their actions and inactions. The reasons behind nonperformance of our elected representatives are that the people (electorate) who are saddled with power to elect them are not informed. The electorate should be politically aware when and how to elect credible people and to know that those to be elected should be people of unquestionable character, anything short of that should be discourage.

The Need for Seasoned Politicians

The Nigerian political developments usually describe the forefront nationalists as fighters for freedom and emancipation of the citizens through their protests of domination and high-handedness of the colonial masters. In these, they usually adopt and use seasoned arguments with support from local and foreign logic, thesaurus, and wise sayings. The nationalists employed public enlightenment and mobilizations against colonial domination and subservience, but there were never violence or bloodletting in the historic acts. The above description of the hero's means that Nigeria needs seasoned politicians to move our democracy forward. The problem of the nonperformance of those who hold political position in this country is because they are not seasoned politician. Supposedly, a seasoned politician is a man or woman who puts public interest first before anything he or she is doing, and he or she must be of unquestionable character.

Nigerian should look forward for a seasoned politician to champion the course of the nation through educational, technological, and political development to fight for the eradication of poverty, corruption, and all kinds of social vices and to put an end to nepotism, injustice, and wickedness that has become custom in the running of the nation. A seasoned politician must be that citizen who will not follow the foot step of "winners take all" ways politics as being presently run in Nigeria. Nigeria needs a seasoned politician who will ensure that equity, fairness, justice, discipline, and rule of law is in place in all aspect of public institutions. The nation needs seasoned politicians to change the system as being presently run now.

What Are the Powers of the National Assembly?

The National Assembly is invested with power to make law that will govern the nation. According to the constitution stipulated as follows:

1. The legislative powers of the Federal Republic of Nigeria shall be vested in a National Assembly for the Federation, which shall consist of a Senate and a House of Representatives.

2. The National Assembly shall have power to make laws for the peace, order, and good government of the federation or any part thereof with respect to any matter included in the Exclusive Legislative

List set out in Part I of the Second Schedule to this Constitution.

3. The power of the National Assembly to make laws for the peace, order, and good government of the Federation with respect to any matter included in the Exclusive Legislative List shall, save as otherwise provided in this Constitution, be to the exclusion of the Houses of Assembly of States.

4. In addition, and without prejudice to the powers conferred by subsection (2) of this section, the National Assembly shall have power to make laws with respect to the following matters, that is to say:

a. any matter in the Concurrent Legislative List set out in the first column of Part II of the Second Schedule to this Constitution to the extent prescribed in the second column opposite thereto; and

b. any other matter with respect to which it is empowered to make laws in accordance with the provisions of this Constitution.

c. If any Law enacted by the House of Assembly of a State is inconsistent with any law validly made by the National Assembly, the law made by the National Assembly shall prevail, and that other Law shall to the extent of the inconsistency be void.

The 1999 Constitution gives the control of the resources of the state to the National Assembly. Section 81 provides as follows:

1. All revenues or other moneys raised or received by the Federation (not being revenues or other moneys payable under this Constitution or any Act of the

National Assembly into any other public fund of the Federation established for a specific purpose) shall be paid into and form one Consolidated Revenue Fund of the Federation.

2. No moneys shall be withdrawn from the Consolidated Revenue Fund of the Federation except to meet expenditure that is charged upon the fund by this Constitution or where the issue of those moneys has been authorised by an Appropriation Act, Supplementary Appropriation Act, or an Act passed in pursuance of section 81 of this Constitution.

3. No moneys shall be withdrawn from any public fund of the Federation, other than the Consolidated Revenue Fund of the Federation, unless the issue of those moneys has been authorised by an Act of the National Assembly.

4. No moneys shall be withdrawn from the Consolidated Revenue Fund or any other public fund of the Federation, except in the manner prescribed by the National Assembly.

a. The president shall cause to be prepared and laid before each House of the National Assembly at any time in each financial year estimates of the revenues and expenditure of the Federation for the next following financial year.

The National Assembly is vested with other powers:

Section 88 grants powers to the National Assembly to investigate any matter under which it has powers to legislate.

Section 89 grants it powers to summon any person in Nigeria

to give evidence (this includes the president of the Federal Republic) or procure any document. In the exercise of this, it has the powers to issue warrants to compel attendance, and the warrant can be executed by any member of the Nigerian Police force or *any person* authorized in that behalf by the president of the Senate or the Speaker of the House of Representatives.

The House of Representatives and the Senate: How Do They Relate?

A Senate is a deliberative assembly, the upper house or chamber of bicameral legislature or parliament, regarded as the assembly of the eldest and wiser members of the society and the House of Representatives is the lower house of the country's bicameral National Assembly established under section 4 of the Nigerian Constitution.

The two chambers are saddled with broad oversight functions and is empowered to establish committees of its members to scrutinize bills and the conduct of government officials.

Since the restoration of democratic rule in 1999, the Assembly has witnessed the election and removal of several presidents of the Senate and Speaker, allegations of corruption, slow passage of private member's bills and the creation of ineffective committees to satisfy numerous interests.

In spite of a more than two-thirds majority control of the Assembly by the ruling People's Democratic Party (PDP), the Assembly have been known more for their disagreements than for their cooperation. The present-day president has been accused of being slow to implement policy. Many bills, since 2007, are still awaiting the president's assent. While the Assembly has made strong and often popular efforts to assert its authority and independence against the executive, it is still viewed generally in a negative light by the media and many of the Nigerian people.

The National Assembly has the unique power of impeachment

of judges and other high officials of the executive, including the federal Auditor-General and the members of the electoral and revenue commissions, but due to lack of cordial relationship among the two chambers, sometimes the assembly finds it difficult to check on the excesses of the executive. These powers to remove high impeach judges and other high officials of the executive are, however, subject to prior request by the president. The Assembly (Senate) also confirms the president's nomination of senior diplomats, members of the federal cabinet, federal judicial appointments, and independent federal commissions.

Before any bill may become law, it must be agreed to by the two chambers, and receive the president's assent. Should the president delay or refuse assent (veto) the bill, the Assembly may pass the law by two-thirds of both chambers and overrule the veto, and the president's consent will not be required. The present Assembly has not hidden its preparedness to overrule the executive where they disagree.

Before the president can be impeached, it must be agreed by the two chambers. If there is no cordial relationship among the House of Representatives and the Senate, it cannot remove the sitting president.

The Voting Rights: What We Should Know as Individuals

Voting rights in Nigeria have come a long way from the Clifford Constitution of 1922 that introduced the Electoral College, to the Richards Constitution of 1946 and the Macpherson Constitution of 1951 that introduced regional legislative councils with the election of four out of twenty-eight members as well as the 136 representative members elected from the regional house, respectively. The Lyttelton Constitution of 1954 introduced direct election in some regions emphasizing the one man, one vote concept in Nigeria. The 1999 Constitution of the Federal Republic of Nigeria provides in: Section 77(2) that "every citizen of Nigeria who has attained the age of 18years residing in Nigeria at the time of the registration of voters for the purposes of election to a legislative house, shall be entitled to be registered as a voter for that election."

Section 132 (5) states that "every person who is registered to vote at an election for a member of a legislative house shall be entitled to vote at an election into the office of President."

And Section 175 (5) mutatis mutandis, in furtherance of the above, Section 14 (1) provides "the Federal Republic of Nigeria shall be a State based on principles of democracy and social justice," whereas Section 14 (1) (a) and (c) affirm: "sovereignty belongs to the people of Nigeria from whom government through this Constitution derives all its powers and authority."

"The participation by the people in their government shall be ensured in accordance with the provisions of this Constitution."

The principle of the rule of law, respect for the fundamental rights of man and the supremacy of the Constitution as stated above must be upheld in our electoral process. If democracy is of the people by the people and for the people, it should encourage the intelligence, self-reliance, initiatives, and social sense of freedom by placing the ultimate responsibility of governance on the citizens.

What we should know about our vote as Hon. Halims Agoda put it, "A strong reason for people's refusal to exercise their suffrage in elections has been severally attributed to the maxim that my one little vote will not make a difference." However, history has proven the enormous power of one single vote. In most of these instances, the fate of nations has been changed just because one individual vote "was cast" or "not cast."

Voting is one of the most important rights and obligations we have to exercise as Nigerians. There is no greater satisfaction than going to the voting center to exercise ones right to choose representatives. Incidentally, there are very low turnout of voters in Nigeria and Africa at large due to lack of political awareness on the part of the electorates, and the absence of feasible ideology on the part of the political party. On the other hand, inadequate preparation coupled with lack of implementation of workable/ acceptable electoral process on the part of the constituted electoral body does not guarantee genuine voters registration. However, the participation of individuals in government affairs broadens his interest; it makes the individual interested in his country and gives him a sense of responsibility.

If you think that your single vote is not important and won't make a difference, consider the following:

- In 1645, one vote gave Oliver Cromwell control of England.
- In 1714, one vote placed King George I on the throne of England and restored the monarchy.
- In 1868, one vote in the US Senate saved President Andrew Johnson from impeachment.
- In 1875, a one vote margin changed France from a monarchy to a republic.
- In 1875, Florida's US senators were still elected by the state legislature. Democrat Charles W. Jones of Pensacola was elected by the US Senate by a majority of one vote.

These instances point to the fact that as Nigerians, it is our collective duty to register and cast our votes sincerely, for our democracy depends on it; your vote is the most effective way to make your voice heard!

In modern constitutional systems, the right to vote is one of the fundamental political rights of a citizen. This is provided by the Constitution of the Republic Nigeria, underlining the universal and equal character of the voting right.

The universal right to vote signifies that every citizen who has attained the age of eighteen has the right to vote and be elected.

The right to vote is an active voting right, while the right to be elected is a passive one.

Equal voting right signifies that each vote cast by a voter has an equal value, with each voter having one vote and none of the votes having priority over others.

The citizens exercise their voting right in elections, which may be either indirect or direct, or a combination of both. In this respect, the right to vote may be direct or indirect.

Direct voting right means that voters may cast a vote for the members of the representative council on their own, without an intermediary. In Nigeria, once the legislature is elected, they also chose among them those who will captain the ship of the National Assembly. Voting right means that citizens who attained the age of eighteen are constitutionally empowered to elect the members of the representative of the National Assembly.

Electoral law provides for a free voting right; this means that voters have the right to choose freely among different candidates or lists and to either exercise their voting right or not, and that freedom is ensured also at voting, as stipulated in the constitution of the Federal Republic of Nigeria.

General elections to the National Assembly are regular and early (in the event of dissolution of the National Assembly prior to the end of its four-year term).

In the event of irregularities in the elections due to which the elections already held are nullified, repeat elections are held.

As chapter 5 of the constitution of the Federal Republic of Nigeria read thus on legislatures as follows:

A Composition and Staff of National Assembly

47. There shall be a National Assembly for the Federation which shall consist of a Senate and a House of Representatives.

48. The Senate shall consist of three Senators from each State and one from the Federal Capital Territory, Abuja.

49. Subject to the provisions of this Constitution, the House of Representatives shall consist of three hundred and sixty members representing constituencies of nearly equal

population as far as possible, provided that no constituency shall fall within more than one State.

50.

(1) There shall be:

(a) a President and a Deputy President of the Senate, who shall be elected by the members of that House from among themselves; and

(b) a Speaker and a Deputy Speaker of the House of Representatives, who shall be elected by the members of that House from among themselves.

(2) The President or Deputy President of the Senate or the Speaker or Deputy Speaker of the House of Representatives shall vacate his office -

(a) if he ceases to be a member of the Senate or of the House of Representatives, as the case may be, otherwise than by reason of a dissolution of the Senate or the House of Representatives; or

(b) when the House of which he was a member first sits after any dissolution of that House; or

(c) if he is removed from office by a resolution of the Senate or of the House of Representatives, as the case may be, by the votes of not less than two-thirds majority of the members of that House.

51. There shall be a Clerk to the National Assembly and such other staff as may be prescribed by an Act of the National Assembly, and the method of appointment of the Clerk and other staff of the National Assembly shall be as prescribed by that tab Procedure for Summoning and Dissolution of National Assembly

52.

(1) Every member of the Senate or the House of Representatives shall, before taking his seat, declare his assets and liabilities as prescribed in this Constitution and subsequently take

and subscribe the Oath of Allegiance and the oath of membership as prescribed in the Seventh Schedule to this Constitution before the President of the Senate or, as the case may be, the Speaker of the House of Representatives, but a member may before taking the oaths take part in the election of a President and a Deputy President of the Senate, as the case may be, or a Speaker and a Deputy Speaker of the House of Representatives.

(2) The President and Deputy President of the Senate and the Speaker and the Deputy Speaker of the House of Representatives shall declare their assets and liabilities as prescribed in this Constitution and subsequently take and subscribe the Oath of Allegiance and the oath of membership prescribed as aforesaid before the Clerk of the National Assembly.

53.

(1) At any sitting of the National Assembly –

(a) in the case of the Senate, the President of the Senate shall preside, and in his absence the Deputy President shall preside; and

(b) in the case of the House of Representatives, the Speaker of that House shall preside, and in his absence the Deputy Speaker shall preside.

(2) AT any joint sitting of the Senate and House of Representatives –

(a) the President of Senate shall preside, and in his absence the Speaker of the House of Representatives shall preside; and

(b) in the absence of the persons mentioned in paragraph (a) of this subsection, the Deputy President of the Senate shall preside, and in his absence the Deputy Speaker of the House of Representatives shall preside.

(3) In the absence of the persons mentioned in the foregoing provisions of this section, such member of the Senate or the House of Representatives or of the joint sitting,

as the case may be, as the Senate or the House of Representatives or the joint sitting may elect for that purpose shall preside.

54.

(1) The quorum of the Senate or of the House of Representatives shall be one-third of all the members on of the Legislative House concerned.

(2) The quorum of a joint sitting of both the Senate or of the House of Representatives shall be one-third of all the members of both Houses.

(3) If objection is taken by any member of the Senate or the House of Representatives present that there are present in the House of which he is a member (besides the person presiding fewer than one-third of all the members of that House and that it is not competent for the House to transact business, and after such interval as may be prescribed in the rules of procedure of the House, the person presiding ascertains that the number of members present is still less than one-third of all the members of the House he shall adjourn the House.

(4) The foregoing provisions of this section shall apply in relation to a joint sitting of both Houses of the National Assembly as they apply in relation to a House of the National Assembly as if references to the Senate or the House of Representatives and a member of either Houses are references to both Houses and to any member of the National Assembly, respectively.

55. The business of the National Assembly shall be conducted in English, and in Hausa, Ibo and Yoruba when adequate arrangements have been made therefor.

56.

(1) Except as otherwise provided by this Constitution any question proposed for decision in the Senate or the House of Representatives shall be determined by the required majority or the members present and voting; and the person

presiding shall cast a vote whenever necessary y to avoid an equality of votes but shall not vote in any other case.

(2) Except as otherwise provided by this Constitution, the required majority for the purpose of determining any question shall be a simple majority.

(3) The Senate or the House of Representatives shall by its rules provide -

(a) that a member of the House shall declare any direct pecuniary interest he may have in any matter coming before the House for deliberation;

(b) that the House may by resolution decide whether or not such member may vote, or participate in its deliberations, on such matter;

(c) the penalty, if any, which the House may impose for failure to declare any direct pecuniary interest such member may have; and'

(d) for such other matters pertaining to the foregoing as the House may think necessary, but nothing in the foregoing provisions shall enable any rules to be made to require any member, who signifies his intention not to vote on or participate in such matter, and who does not so vote or participate, to declare any such interest.

57. Any person who sits or votes in the Senate or the House of Representatives knowing or having reasonable grounds for knowing that he is not entitled to do so commits an offence and is liable on conviction to such punishment as shall be prescribed by an Act of the National Assembly.

58.

(1) The power of the National Assembly to make laws shall be exercised by bills passed by both the Senate and the House of Representatives and, except as otherwise provided by subsection (5) of this section, assented to by the President.

(2) A bill may originate in either the Senate or the House

of Representatives and shall not become law unless it has been passed and, except as otherwise provided by this section and section 59 of this Constitution, assented to in accordance with the provisions of this section.

(3) Where a bill has been passed by the House in which it originated, it shall be sent to the other House, and it shall be presented to the President for assent when it has been passed by that other House and agreement has been reached between the two Houses on any amendment made on it.

(4) Where a bill is presented to the President for assent, he shall within thirty days thereof signify that he assents or that he withholds assent.

(5) Where the President withholds his assent and the bill is again passed by each House by two-thirds majority, the bill shall become law and the assent of the President shall not be required.

59.

(1) The provisions of this section shall apply to:

(a) an appropriation bill or a supplementary appropriation bill, including any other bill for the payment, issue or withdrawal from the Consolidated Revenue Fund or any other public fund of the Federation of any money charged thereon or any alteration in the amount of such a payment, issue or withdrawal; and

(b) a bill for the imposition of or increase in any tax, duty or fee or any reduction, withdrawal or cancellation thereof.

(2) Where a bill to which this section applies is passed by one of the Houses of the National Assembly but is not passed by the other House within a period of two months from the commencement of a financial year, the President of the Senate shall within fourteen days thereafter arrange for and convene a meeting of the joint finance committee to examine the bill with a view to resolving the differences between the two Houses.

(3) Where the joint finance committee fails to resolve such differences, then the bill shall be presented to the National Assembly sitting at a joint meeting, and if the bill is passed at such joint meeting, it shall be presented to the President for assent.

(4) Where the President, within thirty days after the presentation of the bill to him, fails to signify his assent or where he withholds assent, then the bill shall again be presented to the National Assembly sitting at a joint meeting, and if passed by two-thirds majority of members of both houses at such joint meeting, the bill shall become law and the assent of the President shall not be required.

(5) In this section, "joint finance committee" refers to the joint committee of the National Assembly on finance established pursuant to section 62(3) of this Constitution.

60. Subject to the provisions of this Constitution, the Senate or the House of Representatives shall have power to regulate its own procedure, including the procedure for summoning and recess of the House.

61. The Senate or the House of Representatives may act notwithstanding any vacancy in its membership, and the presence or participation of any person not entitled to be present at or to participate in the proceedings of the House shall not invalidate those proceedings.

62.

(1) The Senate or the House of Representatives may appoint a committee of its members for such special or general purpose as in its opinion would be better regulated and managed by means of such a committee, and may by resolution, regulation or otherwise, as it thinks fit, delegate any functions exercisable by it to any such committee.

(2) The number of members of a committee appointed under this section, their terms of office and quorum shall be

fixed by the House appointing it.

(3) The Senate and the House of Representatives shall appoint a joint committee on finance consisting of an equal number of persons appointed by each House and may appoint any other joint committee under the provisions of this section.

(4) Nothing in this section shall be construed as authorizing such House to delegate to a committee the power to decide whether a bill shall be passed into law or to determine any matter which it is empowered to determine by resolution under the provisions of this Constitution, but the committee may be authorized to make recommendations to the House on any such matter.

63. The Senate and the House of Representatives shall each sit for a period of not less than one hundred and eighty-one days in a year.

64.

(1) The Senate and the House of Representatives shall each stand dissolved at the expiration of a period of four years commencing from the date of the first sitting of the House.

(2) If the Federation is at war in which the territory of Nigeria is physically involved and the President considers that it is not practicable to hold elections, the National Assembly may by resolution extend the period of four years mentioned in subsection (1) of this section from time to time but not beyond a period of six months at any one time.

(3) Subject to the provisions of this Constitution, the person elected as the President shall have power to issue a proclamation for the holding of the first session of the National Assembly immediately after his being sworn in, or for its dissolution as provided in this section.

Qualifications for Membership of National Assembly and Right of Attendance.

65.

(1) Subject to the provisions of section 66 of this Constitution, a person shall be qualified for election as a member of:

(a) the Senate, if he is a citizen of Nigeria and has attained the age of 35 years; and

(b) the House of Representatives, if he is a citizen of Nigeria and has attained the age of 30 years;

(2) A person shall be qualified for election under subsection (1) of this section if:

(a) he has been educated up to at least School Certificate level or its equivalent; and

(b) he is a member of a political party and is sponsored by that party.

66.

(1) No person shall be qualified for election to the Senate or the House of Representatives if:

(a) subject to the provisions of section 28 of this Constitution, he has voluntarily acquired the citizenship of a country other than Nigeria or, except in such cases as may be prescribed by the National Assembly, has made a declaration of allegiance to such a country;

(b) under any law in force in any part of Nigeria, he is adjudged to be a lunatic or otherwise declared to be of unsound mind;

(c) he is under a sentence of death imposed on him by any competent court of law or tribunal in Nigeria or a sentence of imprisonment or fine for an offence involving dishonesty or fraud (by whatever name called) or any other offence imposed on him by such a court or tribunal or substituted by a competent authority for any other sentence imposed on him by such a court;

(d) within a period of less than 10 years before the date of an election to a legislative house, he has been convicted and sentenced for an offence involving dishonesty or he has been found guilty of a contravention of the Code of Conduct;

(e) he is an undischarged bankrupt, having been adjudged or otherwise declared bankrupt under any law in force in any part of Nigeria;

(f) he is a person employed in the public service of the Federation or of any State and has not resigned, withdrawn or retired from such employment 30 days before the date of election;

(g) he is a member of a secret society;

(h) he has been indicted for embezzlement or fraud by Judicial Commission of Inquiry or an Administrative Panel of Inquiry or a Tribunal set up under the Tribunals of Inquiry Act, a Tribunals of Inquiry Law or any other law by the Federal or State Government which indictment has been accepted by the Federal or State Governments respectively; or.

(i) he has presented a forged certificate to the Independence National Electoral Commission.

(2) Where in respect of any person who has been-

(a) adjudged to be a lunatic;

(b) declared to be of unsound mind;

(c) sentenced to death or imprisonment; or

(d) adjudged or declared bankrupt, any appeal against the decision is pending in any court of law in accordance with any law in force in Nigeria, subsection (1) of the section shall not apply during a period beginning from the date when such appeal is lodged and ending on the date when the appeal is finally determined or, as the case may be, the appeal lapses or is abandoned, whichever is earlier.

(3) For the purposes of subsection (2) of this section "appeal" includes any application for an injunction or an order certiorari, *mandamus,* prohibition or habeas corpus, or any appeal from any such application.

67.

(1) The President may attend any joint meeting of the National Assembly or any meeting of either House of the National Assembly, either to deliver an address on national affairs including fiscal measures, or to make such statement on the policy of government as he considers to be of national importance.

(2) A Minister of the Government of the Federation attend either House of the National Assembly if invited to express to the House the conduct of his Ministry, and in particular when the affairs of that Ministry are under discussion.

(3) Nothing in this section shall enable any person who is not a member of the Senate or of the House of Representatives to vote in that House or in any of its committees.

68.

(1) A member of the Senate or of the House of Representatives shall vacate his seat in the House of which he is a member if -

(a) he becomes a member of another legislative house.

(b) any other circumstances arise that, if he were not a member of the Senate or the House of Representatives, would cause him to be disqualified for election as a member;

(c) he ceases to be a citizen of Nigeria;

(d) he becomes President, VicePresident, Governor, Deputy Governor or a Minister of the Government of the Federation or a Commissioner of the Government of a State or a Special Adviser.

(e) save as otherwise prescribed by this Constitution, he becomes a member of a commission or other body established by this Constitution or by any other law.

(f) without just cause he is absent from meetings of the House of which he is a member for a period amounting in the aggregate to more than one-third of the total number of days during which the House meets in any one year;

(g) being a person whose election to the House was sponsored by a political party, he becomes a member of another political party before the expiration of the period for which that House was elected;

Provided that his membership of the latter political party is not as a result of a division in the political party of which he was previously a member or of a merger of two or more political parties or factions by one of which he was previously sponsored; or

(h) the President of the Senate or, as the case may be, the Speaker of the House of Representatives receives a certificate under the hand of the Chairman of the Independent National Electoral Commission stating that the provisions of section 69 of this Constitution have been complied with in respect of the recall of that member.

(2) The President of the Senate or the Speaker of the House of Representatives, as the case may be, shall give effect to the provisions of subsection (1) of this section, so however that the President of the Senate or the Speaker of the House of Representatives or a member shall first present evidence satisfactory to the House concerned that any of the provisions of that subsection has become applicable in respect of that member.

(3) A member of the Senate or of the House of Representatives shall be deemed to be absent without just cause from a meeting of the House of which he is a member, unless the person presiding certifies in writing that he is satisfied that the absence of the member from the meeting was for a just cause.

69. A member of the Senate or of the House Representatives may be recalled as such a member if -

(a) there is presented to the Chairman of the Independent National Electoral Commission a petition in that behalf signed by more than one-half of the persons registered to vote in that member's constituency alleging their loss of confidence in that member; and

(b) the petition is thereafter, in a referendum conducted by the Independent National Electoral Commission within ninety days of the date of receipt of the petition, approved by a simple majority of the votes of the persons registered to vote in that member's constituency.

70. A member of the Senate or of the House of Representatives shall receive such salary and other allowances as Revenue Mobilisation Allocation and Fiscal Commission may determine

D - Elections to National Assembly

71. Subject to the provisions of section 72 of this Constitution, the Independent National Electoral Commission shall -

(a) divide each State of the Federation into three Senatorial districts for purposes of elections to the Senate; and

(b) subject to the provisions of section 49 of this Constitution, divide the Federation into three hundred and sixty Federal constituencies for purposes of elections to the House of Representatives.

72. No Senatorial district or Federal constituency shall fall within more than one State, and the boundaries of each district or constituency shall be as contiguous as possible and be such that the number of inhabitants thereof is as nearly equal to the population quota as is reasonably practicable.

73.

(1) The Independent National Electoral Commission shall review the division of States and of the Federation into Senatorial districts and Federal constituencies at intervals of not less than ten years, and may alter the districts or constituencies in accordance with the provisions of this section to such extent as it may consider desirable in the light of the review.

(2) Notwithstanding subsection (1) of this section, the Independent National Electoral Commission may at any time carry out such a review and alter the districts or constituencies

in accordance with the provisions of this section to such extent as it considers necessary, in consequence of any amendment to section 8 of this Constitution or any provision replacing that section, or by reason of the holding of a census of the population, or pursuant to an Act of the National Assembly.

74. Where the boundaries of any Senatorial district or Federal constituency established under section 71 of this Constitution are altered in accordance with the provisions section 73 hereof, the alteration shall come into effect after it has been approved by each House of the National Assembly and after the current life of the Senate (in the case of an alteration to the boundaries of a Senatorial district) or the House of s (in the case of an alteration to the boundaries of a Federal constituency).

75. For the purposes of section 72 of this Constitution, the number of inhabitants of Nigeria or any part thereof shall be ascertained by reference to the 1991 census of the population of Nigeria or the latest census held in pursuance of an Act of the National Assembly after the coming into force of the provisions of this Part of this Chapter of this Constitution.

76.

(1) Elections to each House of the National Assembly shall be held on a date to be appointed by the Independent National Electoral Commission.

(2) The date mentioned in subsection (1) of this section shall not be earlier than sixty days before and not later than the date on which the House stands dissolved, or where the election to fill a vacancy occurring more than three months before such date; not later than one month after the vacancy occurred.

77.

(1) Subject to the provisions of this Constitution, every Senatorial district or Federal constituency established in accordance with the provisions of this Part of this Chapter

shall return a member who shall be directly elected to the Senate or the House of Representatives in such manner as may be prescribed by an act of the National Assembly.

(2) Every citizen of Nigeria, who has attained the age of eighteen years residing in Nigeria at the time of the registration of voters for purposes of election to a legislative house, shall be entitled to be registered as a voter for that election.

78. The registration of voters and the conduct of elections shall be subject to the direction and supervision of Independent National Electoral Commission.

79. The National Assembly shall make provisions in respects -

(a) persons who may apply to an election tribunal for determination of any question as to whether -

(i) any person has been validly elected as a member of the Senate or of the House of Representatives,

(ii) the term of office of any person has ceased, or

(iii) the seat in the Senate or in the House of Representatives of a member of that House has become vacant;

(b) circumstances and manner in which, and the conditions upon which, such application may be made; and

(c) powers, practice and procedure of the election tribunal in relation to any such application.

Powers and Control over Public Funds

80.

(1) All revenues or other moneys raised or received by the Federation (not being revenues or other moneys payable under this Constitution or any Act of the National Assembly into any other public fund of the Federation established for a specific purpose) shall be paid into and form one Consolidated Revenue Fund of the Federation.

(2) No moneys shall be withdrawn from the Consolidated Revenue Fund of the Federation except to meet expen-

diture that is charged upon the fund by this Constitution or where the issue of those moneys has been authorized by an Appropriation Act, Supplementary Appropriation Act or an Act passed in pursuance of section 81 of this Constitution.

(3) No moneys shall be withdrawn from any public fund of the Federation, other than the Consolidated Revenue Fund of the Federation, unless the issue of those moneys has been authorized by an Act of the National Assembly.

(4) No moneys shall be withdrawn from the Consolidated Revenue Fund or any other public fund of the Federation, except in the manner prescribed by the National Assembly.

81.

(1) The President shall cause to be prepared and laid before each House of the National Assembly at any time in each financial year estimates of the revenues and expenditure of the Federation for the next following financial year.

(2) The heads of expenditure contained in the estimates (other than expenditure charged upon the Consolidated Revenue Fund of the Federation by this Constitution) shall be included in a bill, to be known as an Appropriation Bill, providing for the issue from the Consolidated Revenue Fund of the sums necessary to meet that expenditure and the appropriation of those sums for the purposes specified therein.

(3) Any amount standing to the credit of the judiciary in the Consolidated Revenue Fund of the Federation shall be paid directly to the National Judicial Council for disbursement to the heads of the courts established for the Federation and the State under section 6 of this Constitution.

(4) If in respect of any financial year it is found that -

(a) the amount appropriated by the Appropriation Act for any purpose is insufficient; or

(b) a need has arisen for expenditure for a purpose for which no amount has been appropriated by the Act, a supplementary estimate showing the sums required shall be laid before each House of the National Assembly and the heads of any such expenditure shall be included in a Supplementary Appropriation Bill.

82. If the Appropriation Bill in respect of any financial year has not been passed into law by the beginning of the financial year, the President may authorize the withdrawal of moneys in the Consolidated Revenue Fund of the Federation for the purpose of meeting expenditure necessary to carry on the services of the Government of the Federation for a period not exceeding months or until the coming into operation of the Appropriate Act, whichever is the earlier:

Provided that the withdrawal in respect of any such period shall not exceed the amount authorized to be withdrawn from the Consolidated Revenue Fund of the Federation under the provisions of the Appropriation Act passed by the National Assembly for the corresponding period in the immediately preceding financial year, being an amount proportionate to the total amount so authorized for the immediately preceding financial year.

83.

(1) The National Assembly may by law make provisions for the establishment of a Contingencies Fund for the Federation and for authorizing the President, if satisfied that there has arisen an urgent and unforeseen need for expenditure for which no other provision exists, to make advances from the Fund to meet the need.

(2) Where any advance is made in accordance with the provisions of this section, a Supplementary Estimate shall be presented and a Supplementary Appropriation Bill shall be introduced as soon as possible for the purpose of replacing the amount so advanced.

84.

(1) There shall be paid to the holders of the offices mentioned in this section such remuneration, salaries and allowances as may be prescribed by the National Assembly, but not exceeding the amount as shall have been determined by the Revenue Mobilization Allocation and Fiscal Commission.

(2) The remuneration, salaries and allowances payable to the holders of the offices so mentioned shall be a charge upon the Consolidated Revenue Fund of the Federation.

(3) The remuneration and salaries payable to the holders of the said offices and their conditions of service, other than allowances, shall not be altered to their disadvantage after their appointment.

(4) The offices aforesaid are the offices of President, Vice-President, Chief Justice of Nigeria, Justice of the Supreme Court, President of the Court of Appeal, Justice of the Court of Appeal, Chief Judge of the Federal High Court, Judge of the Federal High Court, Chief Judge and Judge of the High Court of the Federal Capital Territory, Abuja, Chief Judge of a State, Judge of the High Court of a State, Grand *Kadi* of the Sharia Court of Appeal of the Federal Capital Territory, Abuja, President and Judge of the Customary Court of Appeal of the Federal Capital Territory, Abuja, Grand *Kadi* and *Kadi* of the Sharia Court of Appeal of a State, President and Judge of the Customary Court of Appeal of a State, the Auditor-General for the Federation and the Chairmen and members of the following executive bodies, namely, the Code of Conduct Bureau, the Federal Civil Service Commission, the Independent National Electoral Commission, the National Judicial Council, the Federal Judicial Service Commission, the Judicial Service Committee of the Federal Capital Territory, Abuja, the Federal Character Commission, the Code of Conduct Tribunal, the National Population Commission, the Revenue Mobilization Allocation and Fiscal Commission, the

Nigeria Police Council and the Police Service Commission.

(5) Any person who has held office as President or Vice-President shall be entitled to pension for life at a rate equivalent to the annual salary of the incumbent President or Vice-President:

Provided that such a person was not removed from office by the process of impeachment or for breach of any provisions of this Constitution.

(6) Any pension granted by virtue of subsection (5) of this section shall be a charge upon the Consolidated Revenue Fund of the Federation.

(7) The recurrent expenditure of judicial offices in the Federation (in addition to salaries and allowances of the judicial officers mentioned in subsection (4) of this section) shall be charge upon the Consolidated Revenue Fund of the Federation.

85.

(1) There shall be an Auditor-General for the Federation who shall be appointed in accordance with the provisions of section 86 of this Constitution.

(2) The public accounts of the Federation and of all offices and courts of the Federation shall be audited and reported on to the Auditor-General who shall submit his reports to the National Assembly; and for that purpose, the Auditor-General or any person authorized by him in that behalf shall have access to all the books, records, returns and other documents relating to those accounts.

(3) Nothing in subsection (2) of this section shall be construed as authorizing the Auditor-General to audit the accounts of or appoint auditors for government statutory corporations, commissions, authorities, agencies, including all persons and bodies established by an Act of the National Assembly, but the Auditor-General shall -

(a) provide such bodies with -

(i) a list of auditors qualified to be appointed by them as external auditors and from which the bodies shall appoint their external auditors, and

(ii) guidelines on the level of fees to be paid to external auditors; and

(b) comment on their annual accounts and auditor's reports thereon.

(4) The Auditor-General shall have power to conduct checks of all government statutory corporations, commissions, authorities, agencies, including all persons and bodies established by an Act of the National Assembly.

(5) The Auditor-General shall, within ninety days of receipt of the Accountant-General's financial statement, submit his reports under this section to each House of the National Assembly and each House shall cause the reports to be considered by a committee of the House of the National Assembly responsible for public accounts.

(6) In the exercise of his functions under this Constitution, the Auditor-General shall not be subject to the direction or control of any other authority or person.

86.

(1) The Auditor-General for the Federation shall be appointed by the President on the recommendation of the Federal Civil Service Commission subject to confirmation by the Senate.

(2) The power to appoint persons to act in the office of the Auditor-General shall vest in the President.

(3) Except with the sanction of a resolution of the Senate, no person shall act in the office of the Auditor-General for a period exceeding six months.

87.

(1) A person holding the office of the Auditor-General for the Federation shall be removed from office by the President acting on an address supported by two-thirds majority of the

Senate praying that he be so removed for inability to discharge the functions of his-office (whether arising from infirmity of mind or body or any other cause) or for misconduct.

(2) The Auditor-General shall not be removed from office before such retiring age as may be prescribed by law, save in accordance with the provisions of this section.

88.

(1) Subject to the provisions of this Constitution, each House of the National Assembly shall have power by resolution published in its journal or in the Official Gazette of the Government of the Federation to direct or cause to be directed investigation into -

(a) any matter or thing with respect to which it has power to make laws, and

(b) the conduct of affairs of any person, authority, ministry or government department charged, or intended to be charged, with the duty of or responsibility for -

(i) executing or administering laws enacted by National Assembly, and

(ii) disbursing or administering moneys appropriated or to be appropriated by the National Assembly.

(2) The powers conferred on the National Assembly under the provisions of this section are exercisable only for the purpose of enabling it to -

(a) make laws with respect to any matter within its legislative competence and correct any defects in existing laws; and

(b) expose corruption, inefficiency or waste in the execution or administration of laws within its legislative competence and in the disbursement or administration of funds appropriated by it.

89.

(1) For the purposes of any investigation under section 88 of this Constitutional and subject to the provisions thereof, the Senate or the House of Representatives or a committee

appointed in accordance with section 62 of this Constitution shall have power to -

(a) procure all such evidence, written or oral, direct or circumstantial, as it may think necessary or desirable, and examine all persons as witnesses whose evidence may be material or relevant to the subject matter;

(b) require such evidence to be given on oath;

(c) summon any person in Nigeria to give evidence at any place or produce any document or other thing in his possession or under his control, and examine him as a witness and require him to produce any document or other thing in his possession or under his control, subject to all just exceptions; and

(d) issue a warrant to compel the attendance of any person who, after having been summoned to attend, fails, refuses or neglects to do so and does not excuse such failure, refusal or neglect to the satisfaction of the House or the committee in question, and order him to pay all costs which may have been occasioned in compelling his attendance or by reason of his failure, refusal or neglect to obey the summons, and also to impose such fine as may be prescribed for any such failure, refused or neglect; and any fine so imposed shall be recoverable in the same manner as a fine imposed by a court of law.

(2) A summons or warrant issued under this section may be served or executed by any member of the Nigeria Police Force or by any person authorized in that behalf by the President of the Senate or the Speaker of the House of Representatives, as the case may require.

Part II
House of Assembly of a State
Composition and Staff of House of Assembly

90. There shall be a House of Assembly for each of the States of the Federation.

91. Subject to the provisions of this Constitution, a House of Assembly of a State shall consist of three or four times the number of seats which that State has in the House of Representatives divided in a way to reflect, as far as possible nearly equal population:

Provided that a House of Assembly of a State shall consist of not less than twenty-four and not more than forty members.

92.

(1) There shall be a Speaker and a Deputy Speaker of a House of Assembly who shall be elected by the members of the House from among themselves.

(2) The Speaker or Deputy Speaker of the House of Assembly shall vacate his office –

(a) if he ceases to be a member of the House of Assembly otherwise than by reason of the dissolution of the House;

(b) When the House first sits after any dissolution of House; or

(c) if he is removed from office by a resolution of House of Assembly by the votes of not less than two-third majority of the members of the House.

93. There shall be a Clerk to a House of Assembly and such other staff as may be prescribed by a Law enacted by the House of Assembly, and the method of appointment of the Clerk and other staff of the House shall be as prescribed by that Law.

Procedure for Summoning and Dissolution of House of Assembly

94.

(1) Every person elected to a House of Assembly shall before taking his seat in that House, declare his assets and liabilities in the manner prescribed in this Constitution and subsequently take and subscribe before the Speaker of the House, the Oath of Allegiance and oath of membership prescribed in the Seventh Schedule to this Constitution, but a member may, before taking the oaths, take part in the election of the Speaker and Deputy Speaker of the House of Assembly.

(2) The Speaker and Deputy Speaker of a House of Assembly shall declare their assets and liabilities in the manner prescribed by this Constitution and subsequently take and subscribe to the Oath of Allegiance and the oath of membership prescribed as aforesaid before the Clerk of the House of Assembly.

95.

(1) At any sitting of a House of Assembly, the Speaker of that House shall preside, and in his absence the Deputy Speaker shall preside.

(2) In the absence of the Speaker and Deputy Speaker of the House, such member of the House as the House may elect for a purpose shall preside.

96.

(1) The quorum of a House of Assembly shall be one-third of all the members of the House.

(2) If objection is taken by any member of a House of Assembly present that there are present in that House (besides the person presiding) fewer than one-third of all the members of that House and that it is not competent for the House to transact business, and after such interval as may be prescribed in the rules of procedure of the House, the person presiding ascertains that the number of members present is still less than one-third of all the members of the House, he shall adjourn the House.

97. The business of a House of Assembly shall be conducted in English, but the House may in addition to English conduct the business of the House in one or more other languages spoken in the State as the House may by resolution approve.

98.

(1) Except as otherwise provided by this Constitution, any question proposed for decision in a House of Assembly shall be determined by the required majority of the members present and voting; and the person presiding shall cast a vote whenever necessary to avoid an equality of votes but shall not vote in any other case.

(2) Except as otherwise provided by this Constitution, the required majority for the purpose of determining any question shall be a simple majority.

(3) A House of Assembly shall by its rules provide -

(a) that a member of the House shall declare any direct pecuniary interest he may have in any matter coming before the House for deliberation;

(b) that the House may by resolution decide whether or not such member may vote or participate in its deliberations, on such matter;

(c) the penalty, if any, which the House may impose for failure to declare any direct pecuniary interest such member may have; and

(d) for such other matters pertaining to the foregoing as the House may think necessary, but nothing in this subsection shall enable any rules to be made to require any member, who signifies his intention not to vote on or participate in such matter, and who does not so vote or participate, to declare any such interest.

99. Any person who sits or votes in a House of Assembly of a State knowing or having reasonable grounds for knowing

that he is not entitled to do so commits an offence and is liable on conviction to such punishment as shall be prescribed by a Law of the House of Assembly.

100.

(1) The power of a House of Assembly to make laws shall be exercised by bills passed by the House of Assembly and, except as otherwise provided by this section, assented to by the Governor.

(2) A bill shall not become Law unless it has been duly passed and, subject to subsection (1) of this section, assented to in accordance with the provisions of this section.

(3) Where a bill has been passed by the House of Assembly it shall be presented to the Governor for assent.

(4) Where a bill is presented to the Governor for assent he shall within thirty days thereof signify that he assents or that he withholds assent.

(5) Where the Governor withholds assent and the bill is again passed by the House of Assembly by two-thirds majority, the bill shall become law and the assent of the Governor shall not be required.

101. Subject to the provisions of this Constitution, a House of Assembly shall have power to regulate its own procedure, including the procedure for summoning and recess of the House.

102. A House of Assembly may act notwithstanding any vacancy in its membership, and the presence or participation of any person not entitled to be present at or to participate in the proceedings of the House shall not invalidate such proceedings.

103.

(1) A House of Assembly may appoint a committee of its members for any special or general purpose as in its opinion would be better regulated and managed by means of such a

committee, and may by resolution, regulation or otherwise as it thinks fit delegate any functions exercisable by it to any such committee.

(2) The number of members of a committee appointed under this section, their term of office and quorum shall be fixed by the House of Assembly.

(3) Nothing in this section shall be construed as authorizing a House of Assembly to delegate to a committee the power to decide whether a bill shall be passed into Law or to determine any matter which it is empowered to determine by resolution under the provisions of this Constitution, but such a committee of the House may be authorized to make recommendations to the House on any such matter.

104. A House of Assembly shall sit for a period of not less than one hundred and eighty-one days in a year.

105.

(1) A House of Assembly shall stand dissolved at the expiration of a period of four years commencing from the date of the first sitting of the House.

(2) If the Federation is at war in which the territory of Nigeria is physically involved and the President considers that it is not practicable to hold elections, the National Assembly may by resolution extend the period of four years mentioned in subsection (1) of this section from time to time but not beyond a period of six months at any one time.

(3) Subject to the provisions of this Constitution, the person elected as the Governor of a State shall have power to issue a proclamation for the holding of the first session of the House of Assembly of the State concerned immediately after his being sworn in, or for its dissolution as provided in this section.

C -Qualification for Membership of House of Assembly and Right of Attendance

106. Subject to the provisions of section 107 of this Constitution, a person shall be qualified for election as a member of a House of Assembly if -

(a) he is a citizen of Nigeria;

(b) he has attained the age of thirty years;

(c) He has been educated up to at least the School Certificate level or its equivalent; and

(d) he is a member of a political party and is sponsored by that party.

107.

(1) No person shall be qualified for election to a House of Assembly if -

(a) subject to the provisions of Section 28 of this Constitution, he has voluntarily acquired the citizenship of a country other than Nigeria or, except in such cases as may be prescribed by the National Assembly, has made a declaration of allegiance to such a country;

(b) under any law in force in any part of Nigeria, he is adjudged to be a lunatic or otherwise declared to be of unsound mind;

(c) he is under a sentence of death imposed on him by any competent court of law or tribunal in Nigeria or a sentence of imprisonment or fine for an offence involving dishonesty or fraud (by whatever name called) or any other offence imposed on him by such a court or tribunal substituted by a competent authority for any other sentence imposed on him by such a court or tribunal;

(d) within a period of less than ten years before the date of an election to the House of Assembly, he has been convicted and sentenced for an offence involving dishonesty or he has been found guilty of a contravention of the Code of Conduct;

(e) he is an undischarged bankrupt, having been adjudged or otherwise declared bankrupt under any law in force in any part of Nigeria;

(f) he is a person employed in the public service of the Federation or of any State and he has not resigned, withdrawn or retired from such employment thirty days before the date of election;

(g) he is a member of any secret society;

(h) he has been indicted for embezzlement or fraud by a Judicial Commission of Inquiry or an Administrative Panel of Inquiry or a Tribunal set up under the Tribunals of Inquiry Act, a Tribunals of Inquiry Law or any other law by the Federal and State Government which indictment has been accepted by the Federal or State Government, respectively; or

(i) he has presented a forged certificate to the Independent National Electoral Commission.

(2) Where in respect of any person who has been -

(a) adjudged to be a lunatic;

(b) declared to be of unsound mind;

(c) sentenced to death or imprisonment; or

(d) adjudged or declared bankrupt,

any appeal against the decision is pending in any court of law in accordance with any law in force in Nigeria, subsection (1) of this section shall not apply during a period beginning from the date when such appeal is lodged and ending on the date when the appeal is finally determined or, as the case may be, the appeal lapses or is abandoned, whichever is earlier.

(3) For the purposes of subsection (2) of this section, an "appeal" includes any application for an injunction or an order of certiorari, mandamus, prohibition or habeas corpus, or any appeal from any such application.

108.

(1) The Governor of a State may attend a meeting of a House of Assembly of the State either to deliver an address on State affairs or to make such statement on the policy of govern-

ment as he may consider to be of importance to the State.

(2) A Commissioner of the Government of a State shall attend the House of Assembly of the State if invited to explain to the House of Assembly the conduct of his Ministry, and in particular when the affairs of that Ministry are under discussion.

(3) Nothing in this section shall enable any person who is not a member of a House of Assembly to vote in that House or in any of its committees.

109.

(1) A member of a House of Assembly shall vacate his seat in the House if -

(a) he becomes a member of another legislative house;

(b) any other circumstances arise that, if he were not a member of that House, would cause him to be disqualified for election as such a member;

(c) he ceases to be a citizen of Nigeria;

(d) he becomes President, Vice-President, Governor, Deputy Governor or a Minister of the Government of the Federation or a Commissioner of the Government of a State or a Special Adviser;

(e) save as otherwise prescribed by this Constitution, he becomes a member of a commission or other body established by this Constitution or by any other law;

(f) without just cause he is absent from meetings of the House of Assembly for a period amounting in the aggregate to more than one-third of the total number of days during which the House meets in any one year;

(g) being a person whose election to the House of Assembly was sponsored by a political party, he becomes a member of another political party before the expiration of the period for which that House was elected:

Provided that his membership of the latter political party is not as a result of a division in the political party of which he was previously a member or of a merger of two or more political parties or factions by one of which he was previously sponsored; or

(h) the Speaker of the House of Assembly receives a certificate under the hand of the Chairman of the Independent National Electoral Commission stating that the provisions of section 110 of this Constitution have been complied with in respect of the recall of the member.

(2) The Speaker of the House of Assembly shall give effect to subsection (1) of this section, so however that the Speaker or a member shall first present evidence satisfactory to the House that any of the provisions of that subsection has become applicable in respect of the member.

(3) A member of a House of Assembly shall be deemed to be absent without just cause from a meeting of the House of Assembly unless the person presiding certifies in writing that he is satisfied that the absence of the member from the meeting was for a just cause.

110. A member of the House of Assembly may be recalled as such a member if -

(a) there is presented to the Chairman of the Independent National Electoral Commission a petition in that behalf signed by more than one-half of the persons registered to vote in that member's constituency alleging their loss of confidence in that member; and

(b) the petition is thereafter, in a referendum conducted by the Independent National Electoral Commission within ninety days of the date of the receipt of the petition, approved by a simple majority of the votes of the persons registered to vote in that member's constituency.

111. A member of the House of Assembly shall receive such salary and other allowances as the Revenue Mobilization Allocation and Fiscal Commission may determine.

D - Elections to a House of Assembly

112. Subject to the provisions of sections 91 and 113 of this Constitution, the Independent National Electoral Commission shall divide every state in the federation into such number of state constituencies as is equal to three or four times the number of Federal constituencies within that state.

113. The boundaries of each State constituency shall be such that the number of inhabitants thereof is as nearly equal to the population quota as is reasonably practicable.

114.

(1) The Independent National Electoral Commission shall review the division of every State into constituencies at intervals of not less than ten years, and may alter such constituencies in accordance with the provisions of this section to such extent as it may consider desirable in the light of the review.

(2) The Independent National Electoral Commission may at any time carry out such a review and alter the constituencies in accordance with the provisions of this section to such extent as it considers necessary in consequence of any alteration of the boundaries of the State or by reason of the holding of a census of the population of Nigeria in pursuance of an Act of the National Assembly.

115. Where the boundaries of any State constituency established under section 112 of this Constitution are altered in accordance with the provisions of section 114 of this Constitution, that alteration shall come into effect after it has been approved by the National Assembly and after the current life of the House of Assembly.

116.

(1) Elections to a House of Assembly shall be held on a date to be appointed by the Independent National Electoral Commission.

(2) The date mentioned in subsection (1) of this section

shall not be earlier than sixty days before and not later than the date on which the House of Assembly stands dissolved, or where the election is to fill a vacancy occurring more than three months before such date, not later than one month after the vacancy occurred.

117.

(1) Subject to the provisions of this Constitution, every State constituency established in accordance with the provisions of this part of this Chapter shall return one member who shall be directly elected to a House of Assembly in such manner as may be prescribed by an Act of the National Assembly.

(2) Every citizen of Nigeria, who has attained the age of eighteen years residing in Nigeria at the time of the registration of voters for purposes of election to any legislative house, shall be entitled to be registered as a voter for that election.

118. The registration of voters and the conduct of elections shall be subject to the direction and supervision of the Independent National Electoral Commission.

119. The National Assembly shall make provisions as respects -

(a) persons who may apply to an election tribunal for the determination of any question as to whether -

(i) any person has been validly elected as a member of a House of Assembly,

(ii) the term of office of any person has ceased, or

(iii) the seat in a House of Assembly of a member of that House has become vacant;

(b) circumstances and manner in which, and the conditions upon which, such application may be made; and

(c) powers, practice and procedure of the election tribunal in relation to any such application.

E - Powers and Control over Public Funds

120.

(1) All revenues or other moneys raised or received by a State (not being revenues or other moneys payable under this Constitution or any Law of a House of Assembly into any other public fund of the State established for a specific purpose) shall be paid into and form one Consolidated Revenue Fund of the State.

(2) No moneys shall be withdrawn from the Consolidated Revenue Fund of the State except to meet expenditure that is charged upon the Fund by this Constitution or where the issue of those moneys has been authorized by an Appropriation Law, Supplementary Appropriation Law or Law passed in pursuance of section 121 of this Constitution.

(3) No moneys shall be withdrawn from any public fund of the State, other than the Consolidated Revenue Fund of the State, unless the issue of those moneys has been authorized by a Law of the House of Assembly of the State.

(4) No moneys shall be withdrawn from the Consolidated Revenue Fund of the State or any other public fund of the State except in the manner prescribed by the House of Assembly.

121.

(1) The Governor shall cause to be prepared and laid before the House of Assembly at any time before the commencement of each financial year estimates of the revenues and expenditure of the State for the next following financial year.

(2) The heads of expenditure contained in the estimates, other than expenditure charged upon the Consolidated Revenue Fund of the State by this Constitution, shall be included in a bill, to be known as an Appropriation Bill, providing for the issue from the Consolidated Revenue Fund of the State of the sums necessary to meet that expenditure and the appropriation of those sums for the purposes specified therein.

(3) Any amount standing to the credit of the judiciary

in the Consolidated Revenue Fund of the State shall be paid directly to the heads of the courts concerned.

(4) If in respect of any financial year, it is found that -

(a) the amount appropriated by the Appropriation Law for any purpose is insufficient; or

(b) a need has arisen for expenditure for a purpose for which no amount has been appropriated by the Law, a supplementary estimate showing the sums required shall be laid before the House of Assembly and the heads of any such expenditure shall be included in a Supplementary Appropriation Bill.

122. If the Appropriation Bill in respect of any financial year has not been passed into Law by the beginning of the financial year, the Governor may authorize the withdrawal of moneys from the Consolidated Revenue Fund of the State for the purpose of meeting expenditure necessary to carry on the services of the government for a period not exceeding six months or until the coming into operation of the Law, which-ever is the earlier:

Provided that the withdrawal in respect of any such period shall not exceed the amount authorized to be withdrawn from the Consolidated Revenue Fund of the State under the provisions of the Appropriation Law passed by the House of Assembly for the corresponding period in the immediately preceding financial year, being an amount proportionate to the total amount so authorized for the immediately preceding financial year.

123.

(1) A House of Assembly may by Law make provisions for the establishment of a Contingencies Fund for the State and for authorizing the Governor, if satisfied that there has arisen an urgent and unforeseen need for expenditure for which no other provision exists, to make advances from the Fund to meet that need.

(2) Where any advance is made in accordance with the

provisions of this section, a Supplementary Estimate shall be presented and a Supplementary Appropriation Bill shall be introduced as soon as possible for the purpose of replacing the amount so advanced.

124.

(1) There shall be paid to the holders of the offices mentioned in this section such remuneration and salaries as may be prescribed by a House of Assembly, but not exceeding the amount as shall have been determined by the Revenue Mobilization Allocation and Fiscal Commission.

(2) The remuneration, salaries and allowances payable to the holders of the offices so mentioned shall be charged upon the Consolidated Revenue Fund of the State.

(3) The remuneration and salaries payable to the holders of the said offices and their conditions of service, other than allowances, shall not be altered to their disadvantage after their appointment.

(4) The offices aforesaid are the offices of Governor, Deputy Governor, Auditor General for a State and the Chairman and members of the following bodies, that is to say, the State Civil Service Commission, the State Independent Electoral Commission and the State Judicial Service Commission.

(5) Provisions may be made by a Law of a House of Assembly for the grant of a pension or gratuity to or in respect of a person who had held office as Governor or Deputy Governor and was not removed from office as a result of impeachment; and any pension granted by virtue of any provisions made in pursuance of this subsection shall be a charge upon the Consolidated Revenue Fund of the State.

125.

(1) There shall be an Auditor-General for each State who shall be appointed in accordance with the provisions of section 126 of this Constitution.

(2) The public accounts of a State and of all offices and

courts of the State shall be audited by the Auditor-General for the State who shall submit his reports to the House of Assembly of the State concerned, and for that purpose the Auditor-General or any person authorized by him in that behalf shall have access to all the books, records, returns and other documents relating to those accounts.

(3) Nothing in subsection (2) of this section shall be construed as authorizing the Auditor-General to audit the accounts of or appoint auditors for government statutory corporations, commissions, authorities, agencies, including all persons and bodies established by Law by the Auditor-General shall -

(a) provide such bodies with -

(i) a list of auditors qualified to be appointed by them as external auditors and from which the bodies shall appoint their external auditors, and

(ii) a guideline on the level of fees to be paid to external auditors; and

(b) comment on their annual accounts and auditor's report thereon.

(4) The Auditor-General for the State shall have power to conduct periodic checks of all government statutory corporations, commissions, authorities, agencies, including all persons and bodies established by a law of the House of Assembly of the State.

(5) The Auditor-General for a State shall, within ninety days of receipt of the Accountant-General's financial statement and annual accounts of the State, submit his report to the House of Assembly of the State and the House shall cause the report to be considered by a committee of the House responsible for public accounts.

(6) In the exercise of his functions under this Constitution,

the Auditor-General for a State shall not be subject to the direction or control of any other authority or person.

126.

(1) The Auditor-General for a State shall be appointed by the Governor of the State on the recommendation of the State Civil Service Commission subject to confirmation by the House of Assembly of the State.

(2) The power to appoint persons to act in the office of the Auditor-General for a State shall vest in the Governor.

(3) Except with the sanction of a resolution of the House of Assembly of a State, no person shall act in the office of the Auditor-General for a State for a period exceeding six months.

127.

(1) A person holding the office of Auditor-General under section 126 (1) of this Constitution shall be removed from office by the Governor of the State acting on an address supported by two-thirds majority of the House of Assembly praying that he be so removed for inability to discharge the functions of his office (whether arising from infirmity of mind or body or any other cause) or for misconduct.

(2) An Auditor-General shall not been removed from office before such retiring age as may be prescribed by Law, save in accordance with the provisions of this section.

128.

(1) Subject to the provisions of this Constitution, a House of Assembly shall have power by resolution published in its journal or in the Office Gazette of the Government of the State to direct or cause to be directed an inquiry or investigation into -

(a) any matter or thing with respect to which it has power to make laws; and

(b) the conduct of affairs of any person, authority, ministry or government department charged, or intended to be charged, with the duty of or responsibility for -

(i) executing or administering laws enacted by that House of Assembly, and

(ii) disbursing or administering moneys appropriated or to be appropriated by such House.

(2) The powers conferred on a House of Assembly under the provisions of this section are exercisable only for the purpose of enabling the House to -

(a) make laws with respect to any matter within its legislative competence and correct any defects in existing laws; and

(b) expose corruption, inefficiency of waste in the execution or administration of laws within its legislative competence and in the disbursement or administration of funds appropriated by it.

129.

(1) For the purposes of any investigation under section 128 of this Constitution, and subject to the provisions thereof, a House of Assembly or a committee appointed in accordance with section 103 of this Constitution shall have power to -

(a) procure all such evidence, written or oral, direct or circumstantial, as it may think necessary or desirable, and examine all persons as witnesses whose evidence may be material or relevant to the subject matter;

(b) require such evidence to be given on oath;

(c) summon any person in Nigeria to give evidence at any place or produce any document or other thing in his possession or under his control, and examine him as a witness and require him to produce any document or other thing in his possession or under his control, subject to all just exceptions; and

(d) issue a warrant to compel the attendance of any person who, after having been summoned to attend, fails, refuses or neglects to do so and does not excuse such failure, refusal or neglect to the satisfaction of the House of Assembly or the committee, and order him to pay all costs which may have been occasioned in compelling his attendance or by reason of his failure, refusal or neglect to obey the summons and also to impose such fine as may be prescribed for any such failure, refusal or neglect; and any fine so imposed shall be recoverable in the same manner as a fine imposed by a court of law.

(2) A summons or warrant issued under this section may be served or executed by any member of the Nigeria Police Force or by any person authorized in that behalf by the Speaker of the House of Assembly of the State.

How Complex Is the National Assembly?

The National Assembly is an institution saddled with power to make laws that govern the state. The powers and functions of the National Assembly are set out in sections 4 and 5 of the Constitution of the Federal Republic of Nigeria 1999 as follows:

1. The legislative powers of the Federal Republic of Nigeria shall be vested in a National Assembly for the Federation, which shall consist of a Senate and a House of Representatives.
2. The National Assembly shall have power to make laws for the peace, order, and good government of the federation or any part thereof with respect to any matter included in the Exclusive Legislative List set out in Part I of the Second Schedule to this Constitution.
3. The power of the National Assembly to make laws for the peace, order, and good government of the Federation with respect to any matter included in the Exclusive Legislative List shall, save as otherwise

provided in this Constitution, be to the exclusion of the Houses of Assembly of States.

4. In addition, and without prejudice to the powers conferred by subsection (2) of this section, the National Assembly shall have power to make laws with respect to the following matters, that is to say:

(a) any matter in the Concurrent Legislative List set out in the first column of Part II of the Second Schedule to this Constitution to the extent prescribed in the second column opposite thereto; and

(b) any other matter with respect to which it is empowered to make laws in accordance with the provisions of this Constitution.

5. If any Law enacted by the House of Assembly of a State is inconsistent with any law validly made by the National Assembly, the law made by the National Assembly shall prevail, and that other Law shall to the extent of the inconsistency be void.

As complex body vested with power to control the resources of the nation under section 81 of 1999 Constitution, which read as follows:

1. All revenues or other moneys raised or received by the Federation (not being revenues or other moneys payable under this Constitution or any Act of the National Assembly into any other public fund of the Federation established for a specific purpose) shall be paid into and form one Consolidated Revenue Fund of the Federation.

2. No moneys shall be withdrawn from the Consolidated Revenue Fund of the Federation except to meet expenditure that is charged upon the fund by this Constitution or where the issue of those moneys

has been authorized by an Appropriation Act, Supplementary Appropriation Act, or an Act passed in pursuance of section 81 of this Constitution.

3. No moneys shall be withdrawn from any public fund of the Federation, other than the Consolidated Revenue Fund of the Federation, unless the issue of those moneys has been authorized by an Act of the National Assembly.

4. No moneys shall be withdrawn from the Consolidated Revenue Fund or any other public fund of the Federation, except in the manner prescribed by the National Assembly.

a. The president shall cause to be prepared and laid before each House of the National Assembly at any time in each financial year estimates of the revenues and expenditure of the Federation for the next following financial year.

The National Assembly is vested with the following other powers:

Section 88 grants powers to the National Assembly to investigate any matter under which it has powers to legislate.

Section 89 grants it powers to summon any person in Nigeria to give evidence (this includes the president of the Federal Republic) or procure any document.

In the exercise of this, it has the powers to issue warrants to compel attendance and the warrant can be executed by any member of the Nigerian Police force or *any person* authorized in that behalf by the president of the Senate or the Speaker of the House of Representatives.

It is from here that the concepts and practice of oversight functions can be understood. During the legislative period of 1999–

2003, some people argued that the National Assembly did not have any oversight functions since the word oversight is not in the constitution. As far as they are concerned, the National Assembly did not have any right to adjust budgetary proposals of the president. By the time it was conceded, National Assembly members could perform oversight functions, another resistance arose, namely that presidential permission ought to be sought and granted before appointees of the president could disclose information to the National Assembly. Eventually, National Assembly could go on oversight inspections. There have been several confusions as to what oversight function really means. Several people see oversight functions as just going on inspection of sites or visits, which are sponsored by the affected. There have been occasions when legislators have attempted to give direct orders to ministries or departments. Certainly oversight does not include the following:

1. Going as a group or individuals to assigned department or ministries to seek for favor, including contracts.
2. Deciding on who gets what contract or employment.

The National Assembly is a large body who oversees the entire governance and should understand that survival of democracy depends on them.

CHAPTER 5

How the Public Views the National Assembly

A Do-Nothing National Assembly

*e*very society is governed by laws, and lawmaking is a higher calling and not a business for derelicts and economic opportunists, says a scholar.

Democracy is a vital instrument that propels political proficiency, economic development, and social stability of any nation state. This is easily actualized where there is a high level legislative efficiency and efficacy. The National Assembly of Nigeria must work hard to be a binding force that will transform the politics and governance of the state into a scenario that will maximally address the yearnings and aspirations of the downtrodden in Nigeria.

There are many knotty issues to address in Nigeria as a nation. The level of insecurity is frightening every citizen. The monster of insecurity of lives and property metaphorically walks the streets of major towns and cities. Most of our roads are short-hand for death traps, while the educational system is in dire jeopardy as standards are fast fading with no one to the rescue. There is need to reposition Nigerian Police Force; the electoral reforms have not made a headway. There is real work to be done. There are power sector reforms, which have been on the front burners. Yet we have a National Assembly constitutionally bound to address the issues stipulated above, but they keep quiet. The National

Assembly members are active only when it comes to matters affecting their welfare such as upward review of their allowances. For democracy to grow, the National Assembly should sit up and address the yearning of the people, to make sure they carry out their functions as stipulated in the constitution of Federal Republic of Nigeria to the later. The citizenry is fading up with the attitude of members of the National Assembly on their approach to constitutional matter/s.

The National Assembly should take action and find solutions toward solving the common problems and challenges facing the nation and its future generation. They should advocate for a return to modesty and morality in a world that appears to emphasize excesses among the rich and the powerful. They should also work toward solving local problems, like youth unemployment, housing, urban-rural population drifts, inadequate and substandard health provisions, and be proactive in solving some of the problems that endangered the living standard of the common man.

The foregoing clearly speaks of the need to reeducate the youths along the often hailed several social-economic reforms that are presently going on in the country (Bennet 1998, Helprin 2001, Forbes 2003).

The National Assembly should behave in way their constituencies will have high regard and repose total confidence in them. The attitude of the present members of the National Assembly on the things that concerns the state of affairs of the nation calls for questioning. This is why sometimes people view them as a do-nothing legislators.

The Great Divide between Honorable Members and Their Constituents

The rudiments of a true democracy are good governance, fair and legitimate elections, justice, equity, accountability, transparency, responsible leadership, political education of the masses, efficient political institutions, and respect for the rule of law.

A good democratic environment creates an atmosphere where elections are free and fair, where legislative seats held by parties are as a result of votes received from the most recent elections and not as a result of cross–carpeting and where, if there is no clear majority in the legislature, several parties may come together to form a coalition government. Hence, democracy is not inimical to any well-organized chosen form of government, but fascism, Nazism, despotism, corruptocracy, favoritism, nepotism, and prebendalism are some profound enemies of equality, liberty, fraternity, and true representation, which are the symbols of democracy proper. (Jakande 2008, 85). Every member of the National Assembly must create a good atmosphere between them and their constituents. They should have a good approach toward the affairs of their constituencies. They should also work to improve the livelihood of the common man in their constituents. Lawmakers should endeavor to know the yearning of their people and work to make laws that will salvage them. Most often there is great a bridge between the lawmakers and their constituents; they will remember the electorate when there is time for an election, promising heaven and earth, which they hardly fulfill.

The National Assembly should know that a strong and vibrant parliament, which has an independent mind of its own, assures the whole society and the outside world that democracy is on course. A strong and independent parliament in our case assures the international community that resources are being properly managed.

Honorable Members Cannot Be Trusted

The lawmakers are expected to legislate for the progress of the nation. They should work hard to make law/s that will promote peace and unity among citizenry for good governance of the nation. In other progressive nations where laws are respected, law-makers legislate to protect the interest of the people. They do this through regular and periodic consultation with the people. Law makers do not contemplate embezzlement of public funds. On the contrary, they get involved in issues like tax cut, increase in tariffs, and pursue trade liberalization, tackling unemployment and other crucial domestic policy issues. It is devotion to legislative duties based on integrity and ability of lawmakers to protect the interest of the masses that distinguish lawmakers from others. The National Assembly is a direct antithesis of what obtains in other countries. It is a legislature that has lost its core values of representation, honesty, and transparency.

The behavior of members of the National Assembly suggests that Nigerians are yet to imbibe civilized values in the art and science of lawmaking. The general impression is that the National Assembly can be bribed to mutilate the constitution. Since democracy is majority rule, majority of the National Assembly members can be patronized to turn the constitution upside down. The attitude of lawmakers in matters concerning state interest is far below the expectation of the Nigerian masses. There exists a very wide gap between lawmakers and their constituencies, as most members seldom visit their constituencies and therefore do not feel the pulse of the masses. The concept of representation has been sacrificed on the Golgotha of self-aggrandizement.

Too Much Gridlock and Partisanship

Democratic practices and good governance flourish in an environment where political elites possess the required leadership skills anchored on the tenets of democracy. It is essential that they represent a broader constituency beyond their immediate surroundings in articulating their respective policies, which derive from a sound knowledge of the rudiments of interest aggregation. The average Nigerian politician should understand the meaning of politics and what democracy means to a nation that practices it. The ideology of Nigerian politicians is far above what is obtainable in other progressive nations. There is too much gridlock and partisanship in

Nigerian political system. Nigeria is a federal political system, a system that defines the structure of the polity in a way that underlines the independence of the federating units vis-à-vis the central government in key areas of national economy and politics. Since the inception of Nigeria's Fourth Republic in May 1999, elected officials, especially those on the platform of the Peoples' Democratic Party (PDP), have contributed to the erosion of federalism by their actions, which have facilitated the entrenchment of unitary practices in a supposedly federally polity. The politics of do-or-die affairs is in the making in Nigerian polity as most politicians applied the Machiavellian system of politicking. This is the reason Nigerians witness kidnapping and assassination of politicians since the inception of fourth republic.

Members Are after the Money

Lawmakers must possess and demonstrate excellent leadership qualities and credentials where they are call to legislate. The question of lawmakers going after money is not the rudiments of lawmaking for good governance. The quality of leadership in lawmaking process determines the incorruptibility, accountability, and transparency of the government. In addition, the lawmakers must recognize their constitutional jurisdictions and the superiority of their elected offices vis-à-vis the diktat of their respective political parties. The collection of legislators in the Fourth Republic (1999–present) is the most corrupt, the least accountable, and the least qualified. This attitude of going after money have made Nigerians to witness many scandals in the National Assembly that led to the impeachment of several Senate Presidents and Speaker. There is no time Nigerians will not hear rumour of bribe scandal by the honorable members of the National Assembly.

Last time the former minister of the Federal Capital Territory alleged that senators Alhaji Ibrahim Mantu and Dr. Jonathan Zwingina demanded a bribe of 54 million naira in order to confirm him. The health care corruption scandal brought down former health minister, Prof. Adenike Grange, and led to the temporary disappearance of Iyabo Obasanjo-Bello.

In a separate incident, a bribery scandal in the Federal Ministry of Education led some senators to tender their resignation as either committee chairmen or members on the floor of the Senate. Those who resigned include Senators John Azuta Mbata (Chairman, Appropriation and Finance), Abdulazeez Ibrahim (Chairman, Education Committee), Emmanuel Okpede (Vice Chairman, Upstream Petroleum Resources), and Badamosi Maccido (Member, Education Committee). The hurricane also swept off the then minister of education, Prof. Fabian Osuji. There were allegations of the MTN bribery. Prior to the alleged scam, MTN gave N4.4 million worth of free recharge cards to members of the National Assembly. However, the three lawmakers were given a clean bill of health by the House Committee on Ethics and Privileges. The matter was not given serious attention on the ground that there was no convincing evidence of culpability in the alleged scam by the accused National Assembly members. In another incident, there were allegations that the House of Representatives spent a whopping N51 billion on overseas travels. There was the N23 million car scam in the lower house. That was before the Rural Electrification scandal that is threatening to swallow Hon. Dimeji Bankole. The level of budgetary indiscipline exhibited by the National Assembly is alarming, and no amount of leadership induced free-for-all fight or intimidation would satisfy Nigerians. This level of going after money by the honorable members is threatening the nascent democracy. Nigerians will not continue to be on learning process all the time. For democracy to grow, lawmakers should imbibe the spirit of statesmanship, accountability, and transparency.

Members Are Accountable to
Godfathers and Not Constituents

The Nigerian political system has witnessed godfatherism among those seeking elective political offices. The case of Andy Uba and Nigige, Mbadinuju, and Emeka offor, all in Anambra State. Adedibu of Ibadan and Ladoja just to mention a few. All these elected officials from lawmaker to governor via president all account to their godfathers not constituents. If democracy is to grow, the lawmakers ought to be disciplined and mature. Lack of maturity among political office holders have left democracy to continue to be on a learning process.

Nigeria democracy ought to experience maturity and discipline, instead what is obtainable is god-fatherism, gangsterism, apathy, nepotism, etc. The National Assembly is expected to change this system of godfatherism in our polity, since they are saddled with constitutional power to make law and amend law for good governance. Lack of good governance has kept Nigeria to where it is today. A good governance system is defined by its relationship to some key prerequisites, including accountability, transparency, participation, and predictability.

Accountability - In a democracy, elected and appointed government officials, from the president down to the office messenger in a local government council, must be accountable for their actions and policies. They must provide answers for their activities to the general population. It is imperative that the population demands this from all government officials at all levels of the political system. One way of doing this is for members of each electoral constituency to construct a performance measurement framework compelling respective government officials to provide answers for their activities and policies. They must demand regular meetings with their respective elected officials at the constituency level.

Transparency - Simply put, transparency is the easy and

unrestricted access of government information by the population. The general public must have access to information on government policies and programs. It is vital that ministers and bureaucrats ensure the unedited dissemination of such information as demanded by the general public, excluding information pertaining to a nation's security. The general public should agitate for the enactment of an Access to Information Act that guarantees the unrestricted access of the public to information on government policies and programs. The enactment of such an Act will compel governments to adhere to the tenets of transparency in their decision making process as well as limiting the chances of government officials engaging in corrupt practices.

Participation - This is a very important component of the elements of governance. It is imperative that citizens participate at all levels of their government's decision-making process. Their participation does not end with merely casting their votes on election day. They must insist and ensure that their votes are counted. For effective participation in public policy, it is essential for citizens to organize themselves into credible interest groups (professional associations, academic unions, students' unions, labor unions, nongovernmental organizations, etc.) that constantly review government policies, articulate the positions of the general population, and engage elected officials in public debates regarding the rationale and impact of their policies and programs on the population.

Predictability - A democratic polity is governed by laws and regulations anchored on the Constitution of the country. Therefore, it is imperative that the application of these be fair and consistent, and thus predictable, within the boundaries of the Constitution. Any arbitrary application of the laws and regulations would vitiate the Constitution and inhibit good governance. A critical element of this is the recognition of the principles of jurisdictional responsibilities, especially in a federal polity like Nigeria. For example, can a federal government establish an act empowering itself to review the finances, policies, and activities of state governments and punish erring state officials?

The lawmakers should be educated, politically conscious, enlightened, and actively proactive to legislate well for good governance and strengthening of our democracy. If they are educated, politically consciousness, and enlightened, they will eliminate godfatherism in our system.

CHAPTER 6

How Can the National
Assembly Serve Us Better?

I f Nigeria attains true democracy, the National Assembly can serve us better. The lawmakers should abide by spirit of statesmanship to work toward uplifting the nation. It is much more settled in scholarly literature that the legislature has important roles to play in a democracy. It is argued first and foremost that parliaments occupy a central position in comparative understanding of democratic experience in developing countries because "it is clearly the key institution in minimal and liberal democracies around the world." According to Bello-Imam, "The legislature is in dissociable from liberal democracies as they are constructed around it or on the basis of it. Any attack against the organization, composition or functioning of the parliament/ assembly is seen as a blow against democracy. Parliament can do anything except change a man to a woman."

Johnson and Nakamura pointed out that "effective legislatures contribute to effective governance by performing important functions necessary to sustain democracy in complex and diverse societies." To them, "Democratic societies need the arena for the airing of societal differences provided by representative assemblies with vital ties to the populace. They need institutions that are capable of writing good laws in both the political sense of getting agreement from participants, and in the technical sense of achieving the intended purpose."

The National Assembly, constitutionally bound to make laws for good governance, should formulate policies that will improve the economy and strengthen our democracy so as to meet the need of the people. Effective legislature works against anything that will undermine peace and progress of the nation.

In terms of democratization, it is explicit in the literature that "effective legislatures help to sustain democracy where it exists and elsewhere help to democratize by fulfilling the promise inherent in the public's right to be represented." Succinctly put, good representative institutions are expected to connect their constituents to their government "by giving them a place where their needs can be articulated by giving them a say in shaping the rules that govern them, by providing them with recourse if governmental power is abused, and by contributing to the procedures and values that sustain a democratic culture." If all these can be achieved, then the public will have moral justification to depend on their representatives whom they have confidence to serve them well.

Minimizing Partisanship

Effective legislature is that which minimizes partisanship in all spheres of the system. In democratic institution, it is important to promulgate rules needed to guide the conduct of affairs of the society. These rules must be made by someone or some group and executed or enforced by some group. In a democratic environment, power belongs to the people who in turn elect those who are to carry out the task of lawmaking on their behalf.

Despite the powers, functions, and privileges provided for the legislature in most Nigerian constitutions after independence, comments and observations have shown that this organ has not lived up to expectation. The Report of Political Bureau in 1987 is more revealing. According to the report, "It is a well-known fact that up until 1979, legislatures were the weakest link in the making of public policies in Nigeria. Between the establishment of the Nigerian Council by Lugard soon after the amalgamation of the Southern and Northern Protectorates of Nigeria in 1914 and the end of the first thirteen years of military rule, public policy making was dominated by the executive. Indeed, a national daily newspaper in 1963 referred to the federal legislature as an 'expensive and irrelevant talking shop.'"

There is too much greed and partisanship among political class, and this has gone a long way to affecting the performance of legislature in our nascent democracy. Our democracy need to be nurtured and strengthened by the political elites.

The National Assembly is expected to build political will, which is needed to combat political corruption, legislative system must foster personal integrity of legislators through codes of conduct for legislators' disclosure of assets, conflict of interest, enacting legislation on campaign, and political party finance; building transparency in wage levels and benefits; ensuring that legislative immunity is not abused; enacting legislation regarding the freedom of information; and protecting whistleblowers. It is important to bring about system adjustment in countries where these supporting mechanisms are absent. The National Assembly should bear in mind that the people who elected them expect them to work toward minimizing partisanship in our political system.

A true democratic system is that which eliminates politics of partisanship, reduces the gap between the rich and poor class in the society, and upholds the dignity and integrity of individuals in the state.

The Presidency and the National Assembly Should Consult More

True democracy has to do with good governance and effective leadership. For Nigeria to attain this, there is need to consult citizenry in captaining the ship of the nation. Democracy thrives when there is good understanding between the electorate and the elected.

Nigeria cannot hope to survive as a nation unless it is able to produce leaders of the right quality and caliber to guide its affairs. This is true of all countries. A Constitution, which fails to throw up the right type of leaders from time to time, may well be regarded as inadequate for one of the most vital of the objectives it is designed to achieve. On the other hand, the Constitution does not make the leaders. It merely lays down the rules for their selection and the regulation of their conduct and activities as trustees of power within the state. A Constitution, however perfect, cannot be regarded as a vehicle for selecting the most capable leaders to conduct the affairs of state. The democratic system ensures that the selection shall be made by the people themselves or by their accredited representatives, and in this sense, the ultimate responsibility for ensuring quality rests with the people. Any failure to choose persons of the right quality must therefore be the fault of the electorate and not of Constitution. The Constitution can help by providing for the disqualification of persons who have been found guilty of offences involving corruption or dishonesty from being elected or appointed to the legislature or other public office. The problem of ensuring the selection of leaders of quality is, in my view, intimately bound up with that of seeing to it that the electorates are given all possible help and facilities to exercise enlightened judgment. This implies that development in the field of education must be accelerated. The presidency and the National Assembly must from time to time consult the stakeholders and other people that matters in the affairs of Nigeria on issues that will bring unity and progress of the country. In making laws and executing it, they supposed to have close contact with their constituencies to discover the yearning of the people and attain to it.

True National Assembly Oversight

Oversight functions consist essentially, among others of examination of the activities of the agency or department in its entirety, to ascertain whether it has achieved the goals set for it. In other words, the examination of the effectiveness efficiency and adequacy of the administration of the department or agency. It also seeks to study the processes within such an organization to ascertain whether due process of the law has been followed.

When the National Assembly was inaugurated in 1999, the atmosphere was not conducive for its proper functioning. The situation was compounded by the fact that there was no precedence, and the bitter conflicts, which resulted in the change of the leaderships of the National Assembly, did not provide the atmosphere for proper discussions. The rancor provided cover for members to shy away from their constitutional and legislative functions.

The National Assembly itself did not have staff with the proper training and qualifications to handle legislative processes. Secondly, members of the National Assembly largely failed to employ staff with the requisite experience and training to be their legislative aids. Some did not even employ and staff. The National Assembly Service Commission, which was legislated into being in the year 2000, had remedied the situation by recruiting new staff and requiring legislators to employ qualified staff, whose tenure security and employments are now guaranteed.

The National Assembly had provided for constituency officers and make money available for this. Running a constituency office is not luxury. Constituency offices must not be just decoration for members. They need to be set up and put to proper use.

Furthermore, the practice in the period 1999–2003 was to exclude legislative aides from committee meetings. They where reduced to bag-carrying staff, and not as research assistants.

The National Assembly should make sure the oversight in all ramifications all arms of government within the ambit of their power for effective governance and good legislation.

Enforcing Ethics Laws

Ethics is a code of civilized principled tabled down to guide every member of the society.

Nigeria's yearnings have been an ideal sociopolitical environment as reflected in 1999 Constitution of the Federal Republic of Nigeria. The constitution outlined the fundamental of rights of individual, organization, and agencies. The National Assembly as a matter of urgency should enforced ethical laws for accountability, transparency, and good governance.

These ethics laws should be enforced so that those in concern will in no measure carry out the fundamental obligations of government toward the people, political, economic, social, and educational settings, etc.

The National Assembly Should Be More Proactive as Opposed to Reactive

Although legislatures are known primarily as lawmaking bodies, it is important to recognize that these institutions have many other important responsibilities, despite what various authors state as the definition of legislatures.

The first and foremost characteristic of a legislature is its intrinsic link to the citizens of the nation or state—*representation.* As John Stuart Mill wrote in 1862, in a representative democracy, the legislature acts as the eyes, ears, and voice of the people: "[T]he proper office of a representative assembly is to watch and control the government: to throw the light of publicity on its acts, to compel a full exposition and justification of all of them which any one considers questionable; to censure them if found condemnable. Legislatures adopt policies and make laws through the process of deliberation. While usually based on some broad set of principles contained in written and unwritten constitutions, decisions need not proceed from the rule of law or specific legal precedents."

The process and quality of policy formulation and implementation are critical elements in determining the level of engagement of the population and measuring the quality of governance of the society should be the yardstick of the National Assembly. The National Assembly should work more to be proactive in carrying out legislation for the purpose of good governance and unity of the nation.

The National Assembly should be proactive in providing an outlet for, and representation of, the legitimate opposition. They should be proactive in striking a balance between an appropriate role for the minority and the legitimate right of the majority to act as another one of those inherent dilemmas in a democratic legislature. The National Assembly should be proactive, open, and accessible organization in the entire political process, for its role is to listen to and represent all the forces, big and small, in the society.

Advocate More Purposeful Spending

The National Assembly should advocate for more purposeful spending in other to strengthen democracy, because no legislature can be effective unless it has adequate resources to conduct research on policy issues, develop models, analyze data, and write laws. The legislatures should advocate more funds on integrated and holistic national security policy framework, which must be predicated on the protection and preservation of core national values, goals, and interests of Nigeria. These values are democracy, the rule of law, good governance, and human liberty (freedom from the erosion of the political, economic, and social values), which are essential to the quality of life in Nigeria.

They should make case for purposeful funds on education, agriculture, infrastructural development, etc. Essentially, the role of the legislature in the budget process can be broadly categorized into two. Firstly, it examines how the government plans to spend public funds and, secondly, how the government has spent public funds.

According to Hamalai, the significance of legislative involvement in the budget process lies in the need to counterbalance executive dominance, broaden the budget process to capture wide array of interests to include opposition parties and constituencies, legitimize the budget process, ensure effective implementation through oversight roles to promote balanced economic development, prioritization, and inclusion of range of social needs and act as a buffer between the government and the people thereby strengthening the democratic process in Nigeria.

Relate to Constituencies More

The emerging conclusions from studies on democratic governance all over the world as well as experience from elsewhere with regard to the practice of democracy show that it is replete with serious problems everywhere. Diamond observed aptly that "democracy is the most widely admired type of political system but also the most difficult to sustain." In view of all these, the members of the National Assembly should relate to their constituencies more to know their yearning and finding ways to fulfilling them. To relate more to their constituencies is the fruit of good democratic dividend, in that process they will get what is needed to make good laws for good governance. Relating well with their constituencies will make them struggle to consolidate democratic institutions and the rule of law, reduce rampart corruption, and boost public confidence in the democratic transition.

The restoration of constitutional rule in May 1999 heralded the new democratic order in which the numerous challenges of demo-cratic governance and development facing Nigeria were expected to be effectively addressed.

These challenges, which are peculiar to developing African countries, include, according to Ibeanu and Egwu, strengthening the basic institutions of democracy and governance such as the legislature, the sanctity of separation of powers and the rule of law, reducing corruption in the public and political spheres, transparency in the electoral system, and the conduct of free, fair, and credible elections.

Even late President Umaru Yar'Adua confirmed the challenges of Nigeria's nascent democracy to Yar'Adua. "As a nation, one of our greatest challenges has been the evolvement of a culture of disrespect for the rule of law...unbridled corruption, endemic crime, violence, infrastructural deficit, and a general malaise in the polity. All these constituted a direct manifestation of disrespect for law and order. In other words, for National Assembly to foster the growth of democracy and achieve legislative goals, there is need for them to relate more to their constituencies."

Carry Out Functions Fiercely

According to Emma Obasi and company on Citizens Education for Nigerian Students, he states that the legislature has traditional right of making laws that govern the entire nation, and members have the power to amend the constitution of the country where need arises. Public Forum: To serve as an open forum for the expression of public opinion, they have a semi judicial function to control the activities of the executive and other branches of government through legislative investigation committee, as the controller of and approval of government expenditure and revenue, and as the custodian of law who gives approval for senior appointments. They are the vital machinery of government who is bestowed with power to make laws effective and good governance of the country. They should carry out their functions fiercely so as to ensure effective legislation, good governance, accountability, and transparency. The National Assembly should ensure that equity, transparency, and accountability reign in all spheres of government.

Accountability in the sense that they should ensure that elected and appointed government officials, from the president down to the office messenger in a local government council, must be accountable for their actions and policies. They must provide answers for their activities to the general population.

Transparency, to ensure that the general public must have access to information on government policies and programs. It is vital that ministers and bureaucrats ensure the unedited dissemination of such information as demanded by the general public, excluding information pertaining to a nation's security. The general public should agitate for the enactment of an Access to Information Act that guarantees the unrestricted access of the public to information on government policies and programs.

Put the Nation First in All
Decision-Making Processes

According to some scholar, legislature emerged as a result of the need for people to run their affairs. It arose from the need to make government accountable to the people. This need for accountability has ensured that all activities of parliament are open to public scrutiny. Parliamentary processes have evolved around openness and accountability. Parliamentary processes actually open up all governmental affairs for public scrutiny. The legislature as the representative of the people is also expected to follow up its legislations to make sure that they are obeyed or are flawless, hence, the oversight function, which gives the legislature the needed information to amend or strengthen or even abolish laws. In view of all this, legislature in taking decision should put the nation's interest first when taking a decision. Most often, Nigerians are worried about the kinds of system we are operating since the elected members of the National Assembly find it difficult to pass budgetary laws as when due, which in effect affects the smooth-running of the nation. They should as a matter of fact consult their constituencies often to get information about them to know what and what their needs are in order to reflect it in their decision-making. The leadership of the National Assembly must always remember why the parliaments arose in the first place and must make sure the dividends of the democracy are down to the people. A strong and vibrant parliament, which has an independent mind of its own, assures the whole society and the outside world that democracy is on course. A strong and independent parliament in our case assures the international community that resources are being properly managed. This will be proper when they put the interest of all in the decision-making process.

Duties by Members Should Be Service above Self

The National Assembly, as the custodians of law, shall by all means prove that they have civilized value in the science and arts of lawmaking. To prove to the whole nation that their service is above self by being up and doing the art of lawmaking. The leadership should prove to Nigerians that theirs is business of mature, intelligent, and honorable men of repute in the art and science of lawmaking. In good democratic nations, lawmakers legislate to protect the interest of the people, legislate to tackle unemployment, infrastructural development, and all those things that uplift the life of common man in the street, and bring the development to all spheres of the society.

For Nigeria to attain a good democratic process, the lawmakers should be mature, intelligent, and honorable men who sees service as above self so as to address the issues of insecurity plaguing the nation at large and work toward strengthening our electoral system. Be service above self to determine how the nation's policies and programs are to be administered. As O. Igho Natufe wrote, "The people of Nigeria share a collective identity as *Nigerians,* they are by no means united in their prism of Nigeria. The shared collective identity is merely a geographical descriptor of their location within a state in the international system, and does not reflect any concerted stratagem to mould a *Nigerian.* Therefore, the citizens of Nigeria are more comfortable identifying themselves as Angas, Bini, Efik, Esan, Fulani, Hausa, Ibibio, Idoma, Igbo, Ijaw, Isoko, Itsekiri, Kalabari, Kanuri, Nupe, Okpe, Tiv, Urhobo, Yoruba, etc. These are the *nations* of Nigeria. They are hardly collaborative nations, but intensely confrontational and hostile in their political discourse as a result of the failure of the Nigerian state to construct a viable strategy of national integration."

Service above self will make the National Assembly recognize all the facts as stated by Igho Natufe and work toward strengthening the unity of the nation by legislating to abide by the rules of federal character as tabled down in the constitution of Federal Republic of Nigeria.

CHAPTER 7

Strengthening Representative Democracy—A Prelude to Good Civic Participation

Our Views to Honorable Members

Most often the legislators displayed affluence without regard to the prevailing poverty in the country. They exhibited this through quest for furniture allowance to wardrobe allowances and many others. This is why most often they are enmeshed in profound scandals that one will start to question what kind of honorable members do we have?

The National Assembly should work toward providing social infrastructures for the citizenry with a radical creation of employment opportunities, better schools, medical services, pipe-borne water, good roads, uninterrupted power supply, better communication system, and effective resource management. If the lawmakers make this available, the eligible voters will have confidence in them as true democratic personnel who make laws for transparency, accountability, and good governance.

As Nwanolue and Ojukwu Uche state thus, "The extents to which democracy and legislative practices are advanced in Nigeria will remain a function of the degree to which the people in elective positions imbibe the culture of constitutionalism. The National

Assembly has however, not succeeded in using its powers to ensure the survival of democracy in Nigeria, considering the nature and character of bills they passed, which had no implicit and explicit effects on the citizenry." The citizenry sometimes sees the National Assembly as good-for-nothing lawmakers who do not put the interest of the public at large into consideration but what goes into their pocket, which supports the notion and reasons why the legislators failed to legislate well for the purpose of good governance, accountability, transparency, and justice.

Involvement Is Key

All hands must be on deck if democracy is to grow in Nigeria. Failure of subsequent National Assembly has degenerated Nigerian democratic institution to an extent that the masses begin to lose confidence on them because they hardly address all the knotty issues beclouding Nigeria as a country. The legislators are not concerned about the state of affairs of the country and how the citizenry are feeling, but they are only concerned about their own welfare. The lawmakers must bear in mind that they are saddled with power to legislate well to move Nigeria forward, which is supposed to be their yardstick for legislation. The progress of every democratic institution depends on the kind of lawmakers they have. If they have credible lawmakers it means that the state will experience a science of good lawmaking, which is business of credible people. The National Assembly is supposed to be a binding force that transforms the politics and governance of a state into a scenario that maximally addresses the yearnings and aspirations of the downtrodden. To actualize this, there must be absolute involvement of all lawmakers concerned. The interest of the nation must be first in whatever they are to legislate. The lawmakers should abolish among them nepotism, avarice, and self-aggrandizement, if they are to make a good legislative assembly.

Holding Members Accountable
by Our Voting Power

The factors behind a true democracy are good governance, fair and legitimate elections, justice, equity, accountability, transparency, responsible leadership, political education of the masses, efficient political institutions, and respect for the rule of law.

Time has come when eligible voters will start to hold members accountable by the voting power bestowed on them by the constitution. The reasons the legislators continue to do what they do is because the eligible voters do not hold them accountable for their inefficiency and negligence in the science of lawmaking.

The reasons the citizenry voted them in is for them to go there and make good laws for good governance, justice, equity, accountability, transparency, responsible leadership, political education, and respect for the rule of law, which is the utmost dividend of a good democratic institution.

The citizenry should recognize the power they have, which is given to them by the constitution to vote in a credible candidate and vote out uncredible candidate. Because if they citizenry exercise their voting power by voting out all those candidates who cannot make any democratic impact to the people, our lawmakers will learn that it is not business as usual, they will buckle up and legislate well so that they will beacon on the masses on another election. The lawmakers should give account to the people who voted them in for good governance, but in a situation where they are there for self-aggrandizement, especially what goes to their pocket, then the citizenry should tell them that the vote is their power by voting them out in any election. Lack of good legislative assembly is what put Nigeria in a position it is today. As Nwanolue and Ojukwu Uche put it, "Democratic environment creates an atmosphere where elections are free and fair, where legislative seats held by parties are as a result of votes received from the most recent elections and not as a result of cross-carpeting and where, if there is no clear majority in the legislature, several parties may come together to form a coalition government." A good legislative assembly provides a good atmosphere for a good election. And good election provides a good legislative assembly.

Swift Penalties for Failure to Communicate

A true democracy thrives where there is discipline among legislators. A good legislative assembly thrives where there is free flow of information. Communication is power they said; information is the strong hold of a good democratic institution. Not communicating well with the society is a sign of democratic failure, and for democracy to move forward, the lawmakers should imbibe the spirit of free flow of information and provide swift penalties to those who fail to communicate when necessary.

A democracy characterized by an ability to respond to popular demands for socioeconomic reforms and an ability to incorporate popular sectors into the political process in any meaningful way is still absent. According to Abrahamsen, this is a key factor in explaining the social unrest and instability that has plagued so many of the new democracies in sub–Saharan Africa. Worse still, the prevalence of a one-party state in order to contain civil disorder and silence critics has led to the formal trappings of multiparty democracy and the declining role of democratic institutions including most importantly, elections, constitutions, parliaments, etc. Democracy must grow to incorporate swift penalties on those who fail to communicate for the progress of a good democratic society. The legislators should legislate well via communication so that there will be no wide gap between them and their constituencies.

Term of Office: Four or Six— What Is Preferable?

Term of office is determined in the constitution of Federal Republic of Nigeria. If there is good governance, there is no need to say four years or six years of term of offices. The reasons people are agitating for term of offices is because good governance is absent in Nigeria system. There is massive looting of government treasures among political office holders, ranging from the presidency down to local government institutions. Nigeria borrowed their system of democracy from United States of America (USA) that practices presidential system of government, and their term of office is six years' tenure for Senate and two years for House of Representative elected positions. In Nigerian constitution, the two houses have the same four-year tenure, Nigeria is expected to abide by that four years' tenure for elective offices as enshrined in the Constitution of Federal Republic of Nigeria. If the system of four years or six is adopted, any candidate who did not perform in four years will equally not perform in the system of six years. Term of governance is not on tenure but on the person who is to lead. If a weak candidate is chosen in an election, definitely, a weak government will be in place. If a weak person is given a mantle of leadership even if given ten years' tenure, the individual still won't perform. Tenure of office is not a factor that determines good governance, but credible people determine good governance.

For government to play its constitutional role in governance, it is vital that it enjoys a degree of independence from the undue interference of a state government. The National Assembly should look into this area and enact law that will give the Local government sector of our democracy autonomy distinct from the state government for development and good governance to strive in our democratic polity. The idea of a state governor determining the choice of chairmen and councilors of local government councils is injurious to the basic construct of free and fair elections that underline a democratic polity. Because of the characterization of local government chairmen as errand boys of their state governors, qualified people with the knowledge, experience, and integrity to manage government institutions are dissuaded from vying for offices at this level. That Mr. Andrew Young, a former United States ambassador to the United Nations Organization, would later become the mayor of Atlanta (that is, local government council chairman in Nigeria) underlines the caliber of leadership and experience that is required mostly at the local government council level. When Nigeria's counterparts of Andrew Young vacate this crucial level of government, then it is inevitable that the least qualified and those more susceptible to corruption would fill the void to serve as militant brigade for their respective state governors. The nature of Nigerian politics dissuades many qualified and principled persons from seeking elective positions at all levels of government in Nigeria. For as long as "Ghana Must Go" bags continue to determine the qualifications for such offices, corruption, mediocrity, and ineptitude will remain supreme in Nigerian politics. The challenge, therefore, is for Nigerians to alter this construct not looking for long tenure of offices.

Any progressive nation that operate four years' tenure, watch out have a good democratic institution. Nigeria should continue to operate the four years' tenure. The presidential system of government from United States of America did not stipulate tenure rather governance in Nigeria is four years, and it is enshrined in our constitution. The debating of four years or six years is not necessary since the factor contributing to good governance is not predicated on the number of days one stays in office.

Good democratic culture must imbibe democratic discipline among office holders and thereby giving way to good governance, justice, accountability, equity, and rule of law.

Yes, We the People Can Govern

The people of Nigeria can govern themselves well if its leadership abides by the spirit of principles of democracy. According to O. Igho Natufe, "Good governance has captured the attention of international institutions, including the World Bank and several inter-governmental organizations like the G-8. Both institutions have made this issue a critical prerequisite in their aid and donation policies to countries with poor records on governance."

He continued, "A good governance system is defined by its relationship to some key prerequisites, including Accountability, Transparency, Participation, and Predictability. Let us briefly review these elements."

According to him, accountability, elected and appointed government officials, from the president down to the office messenger in a local government council, must be accountable for their actions and policies. They must provide answers for their activities to the general population. It is imperative that the population demands this from all government officials at all levels of the political system. One way of doing this is for members of each electoral constituency to construct a performance measurement framework compelling respective government officials to provide answers for their activities and policies. They must demand regular meetings with their respective elected officials at the constituency level. While transparency is the easy and unrestricted access of government information by the population. The general public must have access to information on government policies and programs. It is vital that ministers and bureaucrats ensure the unedited dissemination of such information as demanded by the general public, excluding information pertaining to a nation's security. The general public should agitate for the enactment of an Access to Information Act that guarantees the unrestricted access of the public to information on government policies and programs. The enactment of such an act will compel governments to adhere to the tenets of transparency in their decision-making process as well as limiting the chances of government officials engaging in corrupt practices.

The sovereignty of Nigeria can be sure to govern themselves when fair and legitimate elections, justice, equity, accountability, transparency, responsible leadership, political education of the masses, efficient political institutions, and respect for the rule of law are in place.

Nigeria is a nation blessed with capital and human resources that can be used to make Nigeria a great nation. Our problems lie on leadership and corruption. Corruption is the bane of governance in Nigeria that nobody is escape goat. For democracy to thrive, all hands must be on deck to cage the beast called corruption. Democratic practices and good governance flourish in an environment where political elites possess the required leadership skills anchored on the tenets of democracy. It is essential that they represent a broader constituency beyond their immediate surroundings in articulating their respective policies, which derive from a sound knowledge of the rudiments of interest aggregation. We have run democracy for about fourteen years now yet we are still marching backward instead of moving forward. But thank God we are still struggling to correct anomalies done by subsequent government, but with the National Assembly being stable in making good laws that can move our democracy forward, and then we can say we have all it takes to govern ourselves.

Conclusion

There is no democracy in the world that does not experience in one way or the other bad leadership, but yet they work hard to change the system that make bad leadership for good leadership.

We call ours nascent democracy. We cannot continue to be a baby all the time. We need to grow. Nigeria as a democratic nation needs to ensure that the rule of law and good governance underline political contest in a Federal Republic of Nigeria. There must be transparency, accountability, justice, fair play, equity in all spheres of our democratic governance. The legislature must work hard to put smiles on the faces of citizenry by putting the interest of the country first in their decision-making process. The legislators should carry out their oversight function so as to checkmate the excesses of the presidency, which has been the problem of Nigeria since its democratic process.

The National Assembly should acknowledge the capacity of an individual or group who has done something or contributed to the development of the nation. The legislators should work toward removing callous policies, social hindrances, marginalization, sidelining, injustice, lack of equity, fair play among all so as to move the nation forward.

Since democracy is a vital instrument that propels political proficiency, economic development, and social stability of any nation state, the National Assembly should work to actualize a high level of legislative efficiency and efficacy. We should understand that the National Assembly is a binding force that transforms the politics and governance of the state into a scenario that maximally addresses the yearnings and aspirations of the downtrodden. We should observe that Nigeria democracy has been a mere political desideratum hanging on a limping utopia (Adewusi 2011, 27). Simply put, the National Assembly dictates the operational mechanism of democracy, with certain sharp contradictions arising from defined self interest, instead of democracy dictating the operations of National Assembly. There must be a clarion call for the members of the National Assembly and politicians in general to address the state of unemployment in Nigeria that has deepened level of poverty, triggering off diseases of all kinds.

The rudiments of a true democracy are good governance, fair and legitimate elections, justice, equity, accountability, transparency, responsible leadership, political education of the masses, efficient political institutions, and respect for the rule of law. The National

Assembly as a matter of urgency should be at the fore front of accomplishing these facts. They must struggle to minimize corruption that is ravaging the nation so as to build a strong political stability and promote good governance at all levels of government.

APPENDIXES

The National Assembly and National Development

The recent zonal consultations by the National Assembly in view of further amending the 1999 constitution demands an examination of its structure, functioning, functions and contributions to national development.

Our National Assembly is bicameral: it is made up of the 109 senators in the Senate who are elected at the rate of 3 per state and 1 for the Federal Capital Territory, and 360 members of the House of Representatives. While senators are elected on the basis of equality of states to underline a putative equality of the states and underline the federal principle, members of the House of Representatives are elected to reflect the population in each given constituency in each state.

The basic functions of the House of Representatives are to represent the people by being their voice and arms, approve and amend budget bills, propose motions, undertake investigations and inquiries, amend bills, exercise the rights of initiating government activity and exercise the right to question the government through oversight and impeachment. The Senate, apart from holding concurrent responsibilities as the House of Representatives as listed, also hold the final vote on laws, approves appointments by the president, and approves treaties and such other agreements made by the executive that have a bearing on the international community or other nations.

An adumbration of the functioning of the National Assembly should not delay us here; what is important is to note that their basic nature and functions shape and direct our national life as a democracy.

One very important and sensitive aspect of forming the House of Representatives is a valid and reliable population census without which the democratic principle of "equitable representation" will always be questioned and national loyalty put at risk. In other words, without a truthful population census, fewer people could have more representatives, an inequity which is repugnant to democracy. The House does have powers to regulate executive activity and so, could initiate moves to have a reliable population census in Nigeria.

By the nature and importance of their functions, persons to be voted into the National Assembly should be knowledgeable in other to ratiocinate on the rather deep issues of government and governance which frequently come under their purview: understanding the principles of public service, dealing with experienced technocrats, representing the country in international relations and legations, etc., all these require deep understanding and skills without which the country is sold cheap.

Patriotism is another requirement. A person who must exercise the powers available to a member of the National Assembly must be an altruistic patriot who has the mindset, knowledge and pocket to look beyond self and act only in ways that benefit the people rather than have and act only on the basis of narrow vested interests. He must be a human relations expert who can easily and effectively build teams to achieve purposes that add value to public affairs.

Questions do exist as to whether the principle of "equality of states" can be applied in Nigeria as presently constituted. Note should be taken of the fact that states in Nigeria are the creation of military decrees made without adequate assessment of the viability of these states. In a situation in which the principle of fiscal federalism is applied to the letter, it is doubtful that many states in Nigeria will survive. And yet, it is based on the existence of these states that the National Assembly is composed. The microeconomic and macroeconomic extrapolations of this incongruity have always contributed a burden to both our politics and economy. While the present consultations are going on, a patriotic National Assembly should revisit this aspect of our national structure and take action for it to be adequately addressed.

The powers and duties of the National Assembly make it an important instrument for our sectional and national development and so care should be taken in electing people into it.

Greed and Ethics of Leadership

It was Martin Luther King, attempting to emphasize the chief values for good leadership, that once stated, "May I stress the need for courageous, intelligent, and dedicated leadership… Leaders of sound integrity. Leaders not in love with publicity, but in love with Justice. Leaders not in love with money, but in love with humanity. Leaders who can subject their particular egos to the greatness of the cause."

Indeed, many observers attribute the slow pace of national development efforts to the country's inability to produce and maintain the right leadership with acceptable ethics. It is evident that for more than 60 years, Nigeria still lacks competent, effective and purposeful leadership that could translate its great potentials to real economic, social and political gains.

Nigeria is noted globally for its enormous reserve of human and natural resources, but there is a crying need for leaders of sound integrity, leaders in love with Justice, and leaders not in love with money, but in love with humanity, to pilot the country to it's desired greatness.

Yet this kind of leadership must be far from greed for personal gains, which has been identified as a major negative value that has, and continues to fan the embers of corruption and other ills in most underdeveloped economies, and particularly in Nigeria.

This is even so for as Author Tony Schwartz wrote in his

Harvard Business Review article "Dope, Dopes, and Dopamine: The Problem with Money," describing the power of greed, he stated: "At its most rapacious, greed trump's rationality, judgement, perspective, and any other concern with the collateral damage it may cause." The great danger of greed in leadership can be found in its blinding and pathological influence. It simply urges the leader to acquire more and more for self-gratification without control, and regards for whatsoever implications or consequences.

Rabindranath Tagore puts it thus: "The greed of gain has no time or limit to its rapaciousness...It is ruthlessly ready without a moment's hesitation to crush beauty and life." Therefore, the ruthlessness of greed in any leadership environment, public or private, makes it unproductive, unprogressive, antidevelopment, and totally undesirable.

Experts have maintained that the actions and behaviors, personality and character of leaders are all crucial in helping leadership to analyze what is right or wrong. And since values shape behaviors, the search for national advancement must begin with the enthronement of ethical leadership. Leaders with appropriate values and morals.

According to Complete Guide to Ethical Leadership, "Ethical leadership is leadership centered around appropriate conduct through respect for ethics and values, as well as the rights and dignity of others. The concepts of honesty, integrity, trust and fairness are all critical to ethical leadership." Scholars of ethical leadership identified five key principles of ethical leadership: honesty, Justice, respect, community and integrity.

In view of above definition and principles, greed can be a huge impeding leadership flaw, and an absolute contradiction to ethics of leadership. Leaders are required to personify the collective mission, to lead by example-through words and actions, and to inspire followership.

In the same vain, when leaders become greedy, or dishonest, and lacking in integrity, trust is broken. Credibility lost. This may explain the sundry breaches of the social contracts in impoverished nations, where leaders emerge wealthier and more powerful with little or no credibility from the people. In our fast changing world with its advances, and economic challenges, leadership is constantly under pressure to deliver on the expectations of the people they lead.

The leaders are equally under constant public scrutiny to demonstrate appropriate values as defined by global standards in a digitalizing world. Such public consciousness and scrutiny enabled by global information highway will, no doubt, ultimately force

the enthronement of ethical leadership over the rule of primitive greed in the years ahead.

Benefits of Ethical Leadership Devoid of Greed

Leaders often desire the best from their subordinates but any leadership that fails to demonstrate or promote "normatively appropriate conduct through personal actions and interpersonal relations is regarded as unethical."

Ethical leadership in itself is that leadership that can promote employee engagement, increase productivity and enhance brand reputation as such, organizations should engage in ethical behaviors that can attract customer loyalty by staying true to their mission statements and organizational values Organizations must ensure they have respect for ethical beliefs and values as well as the dignity and rights of others. Doing right at all times, no matter the situation.

Leaders should learn to walk the talk as much as possible especially if they have high expectations for their employees, so, they should lead by example.

Who then is an ethical leader?

He or she is that leader who is always fair and just, has respect for others, is honest, humane, focused on team building, is value driven in decision-making, encourages initiative, and leads by example. In fact, the executive's visibility as a moral person should be based on perceived traits, behaviors, and decision-making processes to define in exact terms who he or she is.

However, where there's no ethics, there would be no sense of ownership and no need for one to work for things that will never be their own. Without ownership, there would be no stealing as people will just take what they want.

One's decisions are often propelled by ethics which makes room for decisions that create positive impacts and steers us away from unjust outcomes. It is usually said that ethics helps make the world a better place through the choices made therefore, ethics should be applied in business just like it would be in personal life.

The aim of ethics has been viewed in different ways: according to some, it is the ability to discern right from wrong actions; to others, ethics separates that which is morally good from what is morally bad; in another way, ethics is purported to devise the principles by means of conducting a life worthy of living.

Operating within the ambit of ethics, problems like scandals, ethical dilemmas, among many other ethical issues can be prevented. It can also help organizations gain more partnerships and customers, which can lead to more money in the long run which is often when the problem of accountability starts.

Just as ethical leadership creates a culture of accountability, greed eats up a person so that he or she is wasted away owing to the enormity of the bad traits developed over time.

Bad traits such as selfishness, anger, jealousy and unhealthy competition which eats up every strand of happiness and may even result in death whereas a simple life of contentment and sharing will lead to perpetual happiness, good health and long life and good business decisions.

Unfortunately, the negative effects of greed on society is the remote cause of some of the insecurity challenges the world faces today; as leaders oftentimes, forget their campaign promises to better the lots of the people and begin misappropriation and embezzlement of the funds thereby, giving room for the not so considerate to unleash their anger on the poor masses since many times, the unethical or greedy leader is inaccessible to them.

Greed affects the world negatively as it undermines the stable parts of the world, which represents human progress. However, a school of thought believes that there are some positive effects of greed on the world such that people continuously struggle without complaints applying the survival instincts that rewards them with good feelings and thankfulness for being alive, not minding the situation. But the effects of greed on social behavior are fundamentally negative as it comes with stress, exhaustion, anxiety, depression and despair. It can also lead to maladaptive behavior patterns such as gambling, hoarding, trickery and even theft.

Greed can get one into many difficult situations which can shorten one's life as greedy people's wants are insatiable which makes them keep struggling to get more money for themselves until they get destroyed this is because, greedy people erroneously believe that they deserve more than others hence it inspires them to manipulate things for better social and economic outcomes than they can have.

Watch out for these traits to know if you are becoming greedy especially with money. Do you allow people you can afford to help suffer?

How hard do you keep trying to make more money?

Are you becoming "overly self-centered"?

How does the rest of your life look? falling apart?

Are you always saying "me, me, me" with very little regard for the needs and feelings of others?

Examine yourself now because envy and greed are like twins. While greed is a strong desire for more and more possessions (such as wealth and power), envy goes one step further and includes a strong desire by greedy people for the possessions of others.

However, if we become more caring, concerned about the feelings of others, have the ability to empathize, or have genuine interest in the ideas and feelings of others, or take personal responsibility for our behavior and actions, our country will be a better place for all and there will be less violence and destruction in the land.

People suffering from the greed syndrome need to find ways to move on from egoistic strivings to more altruistic ones. It's important they recognize that they have a choice. This means stepping back, and looking at other options open to them rather than mindlessly following their cravings for more. Greedy people need to recognize that one can only be rich if one is able to give. Taking this altruistic route requires persistence, patience, humility, courage and commitment. Not doing so will then be at their own detriment.

Then, how can we change the society we live in that believes so much in acquisitions and excesses? For the more we acquire, the more we will want to acquire but if we learn how to overcome greed, we may have a simpler, more meaningful, happier and richer life.

Envy and greed are like twins. While greed is a strong desire for more and more possessions (such as wealth and power), envy goes one step further and includes a strong desire by greedy people for the possessions of others.

It is said that every human being is greedy but the degree may vary from person to person depending on their upbringing. It is therefore necessary that we become alert whenever we feel that greed is blooming inside of us. We should immediately know that our biggest enemy is entering inside our heart and mind and try our best to curb it with lots of effort so as to save ourselves from these two hidden enemies of our inner man through meditation and by reading good books or self-analysis.

Democracy and Free Speech

The federal government of Nigeria in apparent move to control the online activities of secessionists recently suspended the Twitter platform from Nigeria. This suspension has continued to generate public outrage within and outside the country.

Although Business Day publication of June 5, 2021, estimated that Nigeria loses about N90.7 million each hour resulting from the government action against twitter, a platform that has since become a veritable business tool for millions of Nigerian youths. According to US Agency for International Development (USAID), administrator, Samantha Power, there are nearly 40 million twitter users in Nigeria, and the country is home to Africa's largest tech hub. This means there's huge economic price to pay in order to keep the country united.

But this government action does not seem logical in a democracy, according to many observers. For instance, in her swift reaction to the suspension, USAID Samantha Power claimed that: "This suspension is no more than State sanctioned denial of free speech and should be reversed immediately."

This was followed immediately with strongly worded condemnation jointly issued by diplomatic missions of Canada, the European Union, Republic of Ireland, the United Kingdom and the United States of America. The statement is as follows:" The diplomatic missions of Canada, the European Union (Delegation to Nigeria), the Republic of Ireland, the United Kingdom and the United States of America convey our disappointment over the Government of Nigeria's announcement suspending twitter and proposing registrations for other social media." In the statement, these countries went further to emphasize their strong support for the fundamental human right of free expression and access to information as "pillar of democracy in Nigeria as around the world," and stating that these rights apply online as well as offline. "Banning systems of expression is not the answer."

These measures inhibit access to information and commerce at precisely the moment when Nigeria needs to Foster inclusive dialogue and expression of opinion…" They insisted.

Above statements claimed that despite the huge economic loss, the suspension also has diminishing effects on the fundamental rights of Nigerian, and by extension, on Nigeria's fragile democracy since freedom of speech is the "pillar of democracy."

This is equally the argument of those who have stood in defense of free speech. Alexander and Horton (1984), argue that defending speech on democratic basis has many parts to it. One is that the public need to access enough information to be able to make informed decisions. Such decisions and choices can be made in the course of one's business, academics, politics and the exercise of civic responsibilities. The second part argues that since government is only a servant of the people, it should not be allowed to place the limits, or define the boundaries of free speech, perhaps because some governments are intolerant of opposing views and will often resort to suppression of the freedom of speech through censorship in whatever form.

However, it needs to be acknowledged that all around the world, there's no existing society where freedom of speech is absolute. Many experts have maintained that there's need for certain limitations on free speech. The main point of this argument is that speech has to be regulated to reflect the needs and rights of others in society. This also means a decision to define what can or cannot be expressed, not only for the protection of the rights of other members of society but for the protection of State interest. But again, who defines this limit? Should a government sit back and fold its arms to watch citizens publish or engage in hate and inciting commentaries on public platforms without check?

In this, proponents of such position pointed to the Harm and the Offense principles to guide public censure. John Stuart Mills, proponent of Harm principle, believed that "...the only purpose for which power can be rightfully exercised over any member of a civilized community, against his will, is to prevent harm to others (1978, 9), where such harm can be sufficiently established. Joel Feinberg's Offense principle, on its part argues that harm principle is not enough to serve as guide because a speech may offend without necessarily harming anyone.

So what determines the boundaries of free speech needs to be properly debated and appraised before any limitation is established, and this should form the basis of decision making in Nigeria.

This is because in a liberal democracy, any attempt to limit the right of free expression is considered counterproductive and such decision often come under attack as we have seen.

Public Sector Performance and Reforms in Nigeria

Public institutions are departments or components or the machinery of state for executing plans, policies and programs of government. Therefore public institutions here include ministries, departments, agencies, institutions, public funded ventures all under the federal, state or local governments.

It is noteworthy that at Independence, Nigeria inherited a public sector adjudged the best among countries of the Commonwealth of nations. But this is until the first military intervention in 1966, which some experts have accused of injecting its command structure into politics leading to ineffective public institutions and rapid deterioration of government services, infrastructures and facilities.

Following the first three post Independent reforms of The Morgan Commission of 1963, The Elwood Grading Team of 1966, and The Adebo Salaries and Wages Review Commission of 1970, it was The Udorji Commission of 1972 that made revolutionary reforms going beyond review of wages and salaries, and touching on the organization, structure and management of the public services. The goal of that commission was to engender development by optimizing available manpower and increasing effectiveness and efficiency of public services.

The 1988 civil service reform birthed by the Civil Service (Reorganization) Decree No. 43 under General Ibrahim Babangida also attempted to reinvent the public service sector but was met with vehement criticisms resulting in the reversal of most of its changes by Ayide Review Panel of 1994.

Yet in spite of these reforms, the Daily Independent (2009:68), reports that : "At the dawn of the Third Republic in 1999, Former

President Olusegun Obasanjo's administration inherited a public service that had many antidevelopment characteristics; including being slow in official decisions and actions, insensitive to the value of time, irregular attendance at work, nepotism, waste of government resources, corruption, slow change, and irresponsive and discourteous to the public."

This damning report further led to the Public Service Reform of 2004 under the National Economic Empowerment and Development Strategy (NEEDS) with a mandate to create more efficient and responsive public sector.

Yet again, the 8th and 9th public sector reforms came with Presidents Musa Yar'adua and Good luck Jonathan under Vision 2020.

According to Tunji Olaopa in his Public Institutions and Performance of Governments in Nigeria, "The end point of all institutions and administration's reforms is the establishment of effective and efficient public institutions with the capacity readiness to facilitate optimal service delivery to the citizens."

But what is the current state of our public institutions in Nigeria today? Evidence of decay, no doubt, still abound:

- Collapsing infrastructures
- Deteriorating facilities in healthcare, education, etc.
- Corrupt practices
- Poor time management
- Waste of government resources
- Irresponsive and discourteous services
- Irregular work attendance
- Nepotism and more.

This means that in spite of various reforms undertaken through the years, the problems confronting public institutions in Nigeria still persist. Much of these problems seem to derive from poor work attitude and corrupt practices, and this cuts across nearly all institutions in the federal, state and local governments in Nigeria.

While many public servants attribute the problem to governments' poor remunerations, and in some states, nonpayment of salaries; many observers do believe corruption in the public sector, particularly, has become endemic across the rank and file.

However, in April 2019, N30, 000 minimum wage became law in Nigeria after President Muhammadu Buhari signed the new minimum wage bill into law, thus increasing minimum wage by 62.2 per cent, from N18, 500 to N30, 000. This increment negotiated by the National Labour Congress

(NLC) should help the campaign against corruption in public service; even though critics allege it is insufficient in the face of rising cost of living in the country.

A recent investment report from ProShare alleges that, "FG's border closure has continued to worsen food prices; VAT increment, from 5.0% to 7.5%, has hurt disposable income; the removal of petrol subsidy has led to an increase in pump price by 12.4% to N165.0 and electricity tariffs hike by c61.3% from cN31.0/kwh to cN50.0/kwh, have all taken a huge toll on the citizenry. Despite the arguable necessity of these reforms, inflation is currently at a 33-month high with an incredibly harsh impact on purchasing power in Nigeria."

Yet, there's no doubt that any government reform that advances the wages of public servants such as the recent minimum wage bill will help boost workers' morale and performance in the workplace.

Poor Representation and Bad Governance Are the Bane of Development

It is a truism that effective representation is the bedrock of any democratic society. David Plotke, while writing about cold wars in his book Constellations said "representation has a central positive role in democratic politics; for without effective and efficient representation, society will be devoid of democracy dividends" According to Plotke,

"I gain political representation when my authorized representative tries to achieve my political aims, subject to dialogue about those aims and to the use of mutually acceptable procedures for gaining them." This however, does not in any way mean that the representation is the opposite of participation; rather, the opposite of representation is exclusion and the opposite of participation is abstention therefore, rather than opposing participation to representation, we should try to improve representative practices and forms to make them more open, effective and fair.

A representative of the people is, by default, a political leader at the level he represents his people—local, state, or federal. A political leader is that man or woman who represents the people in governance and can only be termed a good leader if he has some sterling qualities such as integrity, ability to delegate, communicates with respect, has self-worth, knows what to do or not do at any given time, can make things happen without stress and has human sympathy, knows when to praise or scold and has the courage to take on and overcome challenges. A good leader is one who has respect for subordinates but unfortunately, present day leaders have forgotten this important aspect of their calling, many leaders today lack focus and so do not produce positive results. Many of them are self-centered and so lack empathy, while communicating, they order instead of interact. They are often fixated in their beliefs and so lack humility or human sympathy and this negates democratic principles or the rule of law.

Without quality political leadership or representation, poverty becomes synonymous with the maladministration that would follow as development is largely hinged on the people's participation in governance just as the standard of living of a people is determined by the kind of government in place hence the need for good governance.

Good Governance can be defined as an approach to government which is committed to creating a system founded in justice and peace that protects citizen's human rights and civil liberties. According to the United Nations, good governance is measured by eight factors-

Participation, Rule of Law, Transparency, Responsiveness, Consensus Oriented, Equity and Inclusiveness, Effectiveness and Efficiency, and Accountability. When all these are in place, citizens irrespective of class, status or group have a sense of belonging; their plights are taken into cognizance and catered for; thereby, giving room for efficiency and dedication.

In Imo State, where millions still live under the international poverty line of USSD 1.90 a day and our government is still battling with the payment of workers' salaries and pensioners' allowances, the time has come for us to assess the actions and omissions of our representatives at all levels of governance. Are they truly our representatives? Can we continue to trust in their leadership? An enlightened Imo cannot afford to be left behind in matters of political leadership.

There is a dire need to change the narrative by electing persons who, by doing of hard work, integrity, selfless and purposeful living, philanthropy and pedigree into both executive and representative political offices.

People of impeccable and proven character should be supported to represent us for when the righteous are in power, the people rejoice.

Imo people should look inwards to support people who have self-worth, can communicate and make things happen without stress. Come 2023, they should jettison money politics and choose the best on all fronts for quality and effective representation.

The Importance of Oversight Functions in Our Nation's Legislative Process

Democracy, the most preferred form of government in the world, depends critically on separation of the powers of the executive, the legislative and judicial branches of government.

The legislature is therefore, critical to making the democratic system work maximally. One of the major ingredients of democracy is to institutionalize government powers in such a way as to ensure that the same group of persons or institutions are not saddled with the responsibilities of lawmaking, law execution and law interpretation. Moreover, it is the obligatory right of THE PEOPLE to "look into" how their interests are being represented and executed by and through their representatives.

This in essence, means that there must be three separate arms of government with their separate sets of functions and powers in a democratic system hence the need to limit the powers of each of the various organs of government remains at the center of constitutional democracy using the instrumentality of compartmentalization of government powers.

Policy representation is often the most important function of legislators since it advances the interests of constituents in the policy processes. In essence, legislators have the responsibility of representing the society through their oversight functions.

What then is oversight? Even though "oversight" and "governance" are used interchangeably, their definitions vary across public and private sector organizations, but they share many similarities.

Oversight refers to the actions taken to review and monitor public sector organizations like the National or State Assemblies and their policies, plans, programs, and projects, to ensure that they are achieving expected results; representing as they should and are in compliance with applicable policies, laws, regulations, and ethical standards.

Oversight is a critical governance function performed by boards of directors, committees, councils, and external bodies so as to ensure that due diligence takes place before key decisions are made, policies and strategies are being implemented as intended as well as see that major risks are identified, monitored, and mitigated, so that expected results can be achieved.

If all these are taken into cognizance, adequate value for money will be obtained, and activities will definitely comply with policies, laws, regulations, and ethical standards.

To ensure that each arm of government performs its role of

governance optimally its powers and functions are divided between distinct institutions and personnel, with each performing some specific but interrelated and sometimes overlapping functions.

For instance, the legislature makes authoritative policies or laws for the smooth running and administration of the state, while the executive implements these legislations or policies through enforcement to give them meaning. The essence of this, is to ensure that the governed are provided good living condition and environment. Therefore, to ensure compliance with the policy content, the legislature follows up during implementation of the policies and measures approved or promulgated by the body which is to ensure good standard of living for the citizenry.

The judiciary which is the third arm of government has its main role as interpreting the laws, as well as arbitrate any dispute that may arise from the processes of authoritatively making and executing government decisions. This is to see that the inbuilt checks and balances mechanisms under the principle of separation of power are in force. Through the power of interpretation, the courts can declare laws made by the legislature unconstitutional, null and void and of no effect whatsoever. On the other hand, the legislature has the power of oversight over the execution and administration of laws by the executive whereas the executive holds the powers of investigation, coercion and implementation of laws and can as well use these powers to call the legislature and judiciary to order.

It therefore, behooves the legislature as an essential constituent of any democratic government and a major factor in its sustenance to promulgate laws to suit the needs of contemporary political systems.

The popularity of the legislature is mostly dependent on the wave of democratic growth across the States, how informed or active the people participate in governance as the legislature is a vehicle for equal and wider representation. What this means is the legislature as the representatives of the citizens could be seen as the hallmark of a democratic government. It should however, be noted that across political systems, legislatures differ in composition and relationship with the executive arm of government.

There is a fusion of power between the legislature and the executive in a parliamentary government, while there is a clear power separation between the two in a presidential government. In spite of these variations in composition and structure across political systems, there are two principles that are common to all legislatures and these are: representation and lawmaking.

It is expected that as representatives of the citizenry, the legislature should not only make laws, but must also act as a watchdog on the other arms of government, especially the executive. In fact, the legislative oversight and representational duties are critical to sustainable development, good, responsible and accountable government for the survival of any democracy and its ability to propel development depends to a large extent, on the capacity of the legislature not only to make good laws for the ordering of the society, but also to ensure that the laws enacted are not violated by the other arms of government hence the need for oversight and scrutiny of administration.

In Nigeria, the legislature has the powers to invite members of cabinet, policy implementation agency of the state and investigate executive excesses or its application of resources to ensure accountability and transparency in government.

This is to say, that the legislature can be regarded as the custodian of sustainable democracy, good governance and development.

Many times, this brings about power play and may be used as a ploy to undermine the powers of the executive or agency deemed opponent which makes the executive arm of government often does all within its powers to ensure its "own people" are in the legislature so as to always be on the same page.

This style more often than not spells doom for development as the legislature many times, overlooks its oversight function just to please its friend in the executive. If well applied therefore, legislative oversight could serve as a barricade against executive recklessness, encourage checks and balances; enthrone fiscal discipline, good governance, accountability and transparency in public offices.

Indeed, the importance of legislative oversight in a democracy cannot be over emphasized, especially in a nascent democracy like ours.

The question is, who can you trust to oversee your interests? A carpet bagger or an altruistic, well prepared, patriotic and intrinsically successful person

Insecurity and the National Question

The recent invasion of Owerri by persons yet to be firmly identified speaks volumes to the question of our internal and external national security. The wave is spreading and for another instance, our own Imo state is threatened and may yet be in the future.

The basic responsibility of government is to secure the lives and property of its citizens. In its own turn, the citizens, on the basis of the Hobbesian principle of social contract, pay allegiance to the government and accept its directives and principles. It follows therefore that when citizens are insecure, their loyalty to the flag becomes doubtful; the foundation for national cohesion becomes brittle and compromised.

The Oxford Language Dictionary defines insecurity as "not fixed or firm; liable to give way or break". Insecurity is a direct threat to our nationhood and emanates from several sources. Firstly, corruption, that invidious and insidious cankerworm that has been the bane of our progress as a people; secondly, bad government which breeds unemployment, poverty, crime and poor health conditions. Third is tribalism and nepotism which kill morale in the public and security services and breed mutual distrust and even pure and unmitigated hatred amongst compatriots. Religious fanaticism and crime complete the list of the causes of insecurity in our society.

Granted that Lord Lugard's foundation for our nation has always been faulty, we have had the opportunity of several constitutional conferences before our independence in 1960 and four republics, interspersed as they were with epochs of military despotism, to correct the directive motives of the amalgamation and forge a strong union of truly federating states, regions or provinces, each being strong and viable on itself while contributing to the federation in an egalitarian and democratic society.

This, fourth republic which is the longest period of democratic governance in Nigeria, should afford us a further opportunity to rebuild Nigeria not minding the fact that it is built on a rather faulty constitution handed over to us by a military hunts which, under pressure by civil society, the press and the international community, was in a hurry to leave the political scene.

A far reaching review of the revenue allocation indices, local governance, control of security agencies, federal character in appointments, educational funding and such other aspects of our constitution will signal a renaissance of the nationalism of our founding fathers and other past heroes. The inequalities and inconsistencies in the 1999 constitution are constant sources of discontent and fractiousness in our polity. A democratic review will restore the confidence of citizens in the nation, douse tensions and foster security.

Our demoralized security forces are another source of insecurity. Poor training, paucity of equipment and poor conditions of service have rendered them ineffective as brigades, hoodlums, insurgents and terrorists hold sway over large areas of our country.

As alluded to above, a constitutional rejigging of our security architecture will certainly take care of instances where herdsmen of no clear origin or nationality can destroy economic crops of citizens without repercussions or legal consequences thereby creating internecine hatred and mistrust.

Free and fair elections, even in a polity of skewed political indices such as ours will make government not only de facto but more importantly, de jure, and therefore more acceptable to the people. Acceptance breeds the respect and attracts the cooperation of the citizenry and so on to stability and security. Rigged elections breed distrust of government and a proclivity toward resistance, contumacy and in many cases, insurgency.

There are fears by sections of our nation engendered by the actions of people in government. When major appointments are reserved for a section of the country, budgetary allocations and implementation favor another part, minimum attainment requirements for admission into academic institutions and public services are lowered for another section etc, a feeling of ennui and apathy is created within the marginalized communities who can easily become restive.

So also will people whose immediate environments and sources of livelihood are impacted by economic exploitation of natural resources but who are not adequately compensated or accommodated in national affairs be irascible leading to restiveness.

It should be clear that the spate of attacks against both government and groups in the country has created an urgent need for appraising our politics with a view to improving our security and giving hope to our continued survival as a sovereign nation. That is the primary purpose of government; all of its stakeholders—executive, legislative, judiciary, and the general citizenry—should be involved and must take it as a duty to ensure security of lives and property.

However, the executive arm of government should take the lead through effective democratic governance supported by the legislature.

True Federalism, Restructuring and the National Question

A federation in its true sense is a state or nation in which constituent parts surrender a part of their sovereignty to a central (federal) government while retaining allocations and laws depending on their own peculiarities. This implies that in a federation there must be a minimum of two strata of government-central or federal and the governments of the constituent parts.

There are several reasons why a federation is formed: geographical location, political history, defense against a common enemy etc. The Nigerian "federation is a result of colonialism.

Is Nigeria a federal state? Every patriot must answer this question unequivocally and truthfully.

Since 1954, Nigeria has presented itself to the world as a federation and each of the constitutional conferences held in her behalf have always recommended this type of government. However, the actual practice of governance in Nigeria renders the "federating units" mere agents of the central government. This accrues because the states (or even the regions before them) had no real sovereignty to declare or surrender part thereof as there never was any social contract entered in their formation. They are creations of the central government through the instrumentality of military decrees. Since a basic ingredient of true federalism is a written constitution, the concept is untenable between states created by military decrees. Under our circumstances, it is only natural that the states are empowered to act as agents of their creator the federal government; and so, we have in truth, a unitary government which, being distant from the people, breeds a sense of alienation by the constituent parts, ethnic loyalty and politics and thence, instability.

In a true federation there is parity in parity between the central and regional/provincial/state government in such a way that the states or provinces can provide their own laws and services to suit local traditional values and situations. The diversity of "nations" with diverse resources, mindsets and cultures in Nigeria demands a true federation. These "nations" or products of "group agreements" should be the federating units with inherent powers to produce and distribute wealth, administer society, educate the citizenry and secure lives and property according to local circumstances. These nations and possible groups are easily identifiable in Nigeria; and they have often presented themselves and their points of view in the constitutional conferences we have had, in media presentations, in voting patterns and political party alliances and, unfortunately, sometimes by violent means.

This is the reason why, in the interest of the unity and stability of this country, the demand for restructuring through constitutional amendments should be given priority attention by the national and state assemblies.

The advantages of this move are myriad and are a compass to national progress. In the first place, it will breed a sense of belonging in each ethnic group which breeds loyalty to the flag which in turn breeds mutual respect and respect of each other and the establishment of enduring peace without which no nation can exist. Secondly, laws, procedures and all social content become local and therefore more easily accepted leading to ease of life and doing business which lead to prosperity. Thirdly, the diffusion of critical and effective power strands to the states makes the federal government not so attractive as to produce the heat, mutual suspicion and antagonism as it presently does.

One important but often neglected aspect of true federalism is election-and representation. Indeed, the personal sovereignty of individuals are transmitted to all levels of governance, local, provincial, state or federal by their representatives who, in ideal situations, must act only as dictated by and in the interests of their constituents. A flawed electoral process is therefore, antithetical to the positions of true federalism. In the same way, interference in local politics by officers of another tier of government is a threat to true federalism.

As already pointed out, the advantages of establishing a true federation are many but its adumbration should not delay us here. What is important is that having recognized this urgent need, action should be taken to ensure that we achieve it in the interest of our nation's peace and unity.

The Quiddity of Public Service and National Development

Governments the world over depend on their public service sectors to operate in their primary and secondary responsibilities of providing security for lives and property and in ordering public life. The public service sectors include all organizations that provide services to people within its jurisdiction; it includes the civil service and, often, is directed by a political leadership. The public service in essence is designed to provide stability and continuity to governance without any objective of economic, social or political profit to itself or its leadership. The public service is always available to political leadership but must act to protect the society from any untoward aim of political leadership. In this way, it provides stability and insurance to the public good.

It is this quality of the public service that makes it the most important tool in the hands of citizens-businessmen, military men, politicians etc.-to foster national development.

In Nigeria the public service is normally referred to as Ministries, Departments and Agencies (MDAs): they exist for the purpose of policy implementation, act as a trust, provide services to people without a profit motive, regulate public life, act as governmental agents to the public, advises government etc. Examples include education, security services, parastatals, government health facilities etc.

Clearly, based on its characteristics and functions, the public service is the lynchpin that holds governance and determines its success or failure. In Nigeria where the news space is replete with stories of corruption, abandoned projects, injustice, election rigging, ghost workers, dysfunctional and nonfunctioning infrastructure, examination malpractices and many other social ills, the public service must be put to question.

No road can fail if the Director of Road Works supervised it diligently and the Permanent Secretary,

The Chief Financial Officer and the Ministry Auditor followed the Civil Service Rules rigorously and loyally; no ghost workers would appear in the local governments' salaries vouchers if the Director of General Services, the Head of Personnel Management and the Treasurer did their transparent bit of work; no grades would be sold in our tertiary education system if the lecturers and examination officers were not corrupt; crime would be better controlled if our policemen were less corrupt as is being presently reported and experienced. The examples of poor or even criminal performances could go on through the gamut of our public services. Much of the failure in Nigeria could have been prevented if the public service was up to its creed and duty.

However, it is the duty of political leadership which is the apex authority in public service to take control of and direct the public service to new vistas of procedures, content and attainment. Modern civilization is replete with examples of how a political leader, party or a group of political leaders have changed the direction and fortunes of their countries: the Buhari-Idiagbon regime, J J Rawlings in Ghana, Mandela during the struggle and renaissance in South Africa, the revisionism of Donald Trump, the humanistic/compassionate style of Biden, the rise of China as an economic and military power in the world. In each of these examples, the political leadership is by well grounded, well prepared, altruistic and patriotic citizens who committed their lives to preparing and dedicating themselves to public service; not carpetbaggers and profiteering social parasites who binge on and take public trust for granted. As we hope to energize our economic and sociopolitical development through an ethical revolution in the society at large and the public service in particular, it is the duty of every responsible citizen to help in identifying, supporting and electing well prepared and trustworthy persons into our executive and legislative bodies so as to provide the necessary moral compass and fortitude that will reform the public service and put it in a position to validly and reliably serve us.

The move is ours to make: rightly or wrongly.

Restructure, Secession: Nigeria's Greatest Dilemma

The Nigeria Civil War captured the world's attention more than fifty years ago. The war which raged in Biafra, the secessionist region in the southeast of Nigeria from July 6, 1967 to January 15, 1970 was the first modern civil war in sub-Saharan Africa after independence and was regarded one of the bloodiest. It was rumored that about 1 to 3 million people died, mostly from starvation, sparking a massive humanitarian crisis as according to reports; the levels of starvation in Biafra were three times higher than the starvation reported during World War II in Stalingrad and Holland.

In spite of these, the war ended on a solemn note: "No victor, No vanquished" what this slogan really means is yet to be fully understood by the common Nigerian as the country is again tilting toward another war as proclaimed in many quarters including former President Olusegun Obasanjo who believes war will soon erupt in Nigeria thus incurring the irk of the ruling party, All Progressives Congress, APC, and confusing Nigerians the more.

With the happenings in the country today, one is wont to say that Nigeria is neither here nor there; for the tribe, religion or class one belongs to, determines to a large extent what side one chooses to tow. While the southerners clamor for separation, the northerners desire restructuring all based on their understanding and what they hope to gain but it is a known fact that the process of evolution or attainment and development of a nation cannot be achieved overnight since it must come with its attendant mistakes, lessons, considerations, concession, compromises, sacrifices, loses, or gains and lots more.

This is no difference with Nigeria as a nation which has over 250 tribes, different cultures and traditions as well as religion hence the seeming nepotism and favoritism in the country that has made Nigeria's political development dislocated and disrupted thereby, decreasing the chances of fixing the Nigerian state despite efforts being made by her leadership.

With these happenings it becomes pertinent to ask does Nigeria require a new constitution? Or do we need to restructure the Nigerian state to address the structural inequities of our system? If the answer to these questions remains YES then we need to change the current constitutional order. Nigeria needs a systems overhaul and a brand new constitution. For we must build a country of laws where there is liberty and justice for all.

It is unfortunate that based on "Uti Possidetis juris" which means the ability to effectively defend one's territorial boundaries, Biafra maybe said to have lost her sovereignty after it succumbed to the peace treaty and failed to defend her territory effectively, during the Nigeria/Biafra war in 1967 thereby, making Biafra territory a conquered territory and by application of Uti Possidetis juris, the property of the conqueror-Nigeria, but is this the reason for the marginalization today one may ask?

Recently, the President Muhammadu Buhari led administration held a security meeting discussing the insecurity in the South East. There were 15 people in attendance, out of which 12 were from Northern Nigeria, representing 80%. Only 3 were from the South, but none of the 3 was from the Southeast. Yet, the main subject on the agenda was Southeast insecurity. This, many viewed as sectionalism, nepotism, tribalism and cronyism.

In spite of setting up various constitutions making and remaking conferences and amendments; establishment of Constituent Assemblies, the problem of sectionalization remains a major hindrance and threat to effective restructuring in Nigeria even though some of the challenges are not new, for they have been there since the pre-independence era, manifesting in different forms and dimensions, there is a dire need to adhere to the yearnings of the people and do the needful else this restructuring will remain enveloped in fear, anxiety, hope, despair and desperation, and promoting the elite" interests in continuous access to power and resources, with firm control and consolidation of same. The Northern Region of Nigeria, which had hitherto, resisted all calls for restructuring is now championing the call for restructuring but still with mixed feelings.

There are however some critical issues that must be addressed for the restructuring to be meaningful and functional. Issues such as conflicts over revenue allocation, resource control, cattle rustling, kidnapping, cultism, armed banditry, attacks on oil facilities and installations, bitter politics of ethno-religious and regional identities, ethno-religious intolerances, poverty, ethno-religious, conspired and orchestrated Fulani/herdsmen-farmers conflicts, unemployment, socio-economic and infrastructural deteriorations as well as corruption. These issues can be regarded as the determinants of Nigeria's future in relation to unity, cohesion and stability among all components of the country.

The elites especially who want to hold on to power or those who lost out in the political merchandise, seem to be the ardent promoters of restructuring even in the South East whereas the masses probably influenced by agitations by the Indegenous People of Biafra, IPOB, for secession stick to their clamour for separation. But the question is: Is the SouthEast ready for separation?

The Igbo political class has however, been calling for a Nigeria president from the Igbo extraction whether this will happen or not is still unclear but many still believe going separate ways remains the best option and many including the Arewa Consultative Forum are beginning to buy this idea but are we ready to go our separate ways? This is because every economic theory of secession predicts that a region chooses to secede if it expects to benefit. Though this basic prediction remains untested it is necessary to look inwards to know if the benefits outweigh the losses before embarking on the journey of no return.

According to George Mason in his 2017 book "Secession and Security", and political scientist Ahsan Butt, states respond violently to secessionist movements if the potential state would pose a greater threat than a violent secessionist movement would. He argued that states perceive future war as likely with a potential new state if the ethnic group driving the secessionist struggle has deep identity division with the central state, and if the regional neighbourhood is violent and unstable.

Ndi Igbo who are known globally as traders with businesses all over Nigeria should therefore, remember that small nations face more costs to trade that larger countries can avoid. Even relatively open international borders impose some frictions but without internal trade barriers, a large country has efficient access to large domestic markets, avoiding trade frictions. Furthermore, larger nations can support more diverse markets.

Based on these, all Nigerians should reflect and act on these arguments in our collective self-interest. Our country is not working. Many groups feel marginalized today or have felt marginalized at different stages of our national history. We cannot even achieve greatness as a country without national unity, stability and cohesion. Many nations have achieved nationhood and prosperity in diversity, which is the default composition of most nations on earth as only a few nations, like Japan and Korea, are truly homogenous so, we can do a lot better if we come together as one in a country where every section or region has a say and equal rights than when we go our separate ways.

Local Government Funding in Nigeria

In the Nigeria federation, the local government is the third tier of government that provides governance at the roots. The local government system in Nigeria derives its existence from the Constitution of the federal republic, as can be seen in section 7(1) of the 1979 Constitution, which states that, "the system of democratically elected local government councils is under this Constitution guaranteed."

Nigeria presently has a total of 774 local government councils spread across the 36 states of the federation with duties ranging from road construction and maintenance, financing of primary, adult and vocational education, health, agriculture and natural resource development.

Local governments are drivers of development at the grassroots, and to be able to effectively deliver on its responsibilities to the people, it is critical to allow them the freedom to manage their resources without any interference from either the state or federal governments. The debate for local government autonomy has been on for many years in Nigeria engaging the attention of media, politicians and the general public.

To fully understand the concept of local government autonomy, we shall refer to experts definition: Local government autonomy can be defined as "the freedom of the local government to recruit and manage its own staff, raise and manage its own finances, make by-laws and policies, and discharge its functions as provided by law without interference from the higher governments (Ogunna, 199: 350). This definition, as can be understood, shows local government autonomy to mean that the local governments must operate as separate entities and not as an appendage of the state or federal government, but must exercise its freedom to conduct its affairs with control.

Sadly, since the inception of the local government system in the country, observers argue that local governments have remained a caricature without any life of their own.

This is largely because of the greed of various state administrators who ran and continue to run the local governments as extension of their political empires. This is also why state governors and their political parties act as demi-God's to decide who becomes chairman or councilor, and in many states of the federation, governors and their parties have hijacked the entire elective positions in the local government councils.

To further keep the local government under control, state governors favored the State Joint Local Government Account (SJLGA), which was introduced in 1981 during the second republic, under Alhaji Shehu Shagari. The State Joint Local Government Account initiative as acknowledged by the 1999 Constitution requires that "Each state shall maintain a specific account to be called 'State Joint Local Government Account' to which shall be paid all allocations to the local government councils of the state from the federation account and from the government of the state." And the Constitution goes further to state that, "The amount standing to the credit of local government councils in the federation account shall also be allocated to the states for the benefits of their local government councils on such terms and in such manner as may be prescribed by the national assembly."

By these constitutional provisions, state governors over the years, have taken effective control of local government allocations, and have been observed to spend the funds in whatever way that's pleasing to them. Therefore, without fiscal autonomy, local governments in Nigeria have been constantly starved of funds, and cannot fulfill their developmental responsibilities to the people at the grassroots.

In 2011, former President Good luck Jonathan, while in office, submitted a Bill to the National Assembly seeking to do away with the State Joint Local Government Account, and to grant financial autonomy to all 774 local governments in the country but the bill was not passed. In 2019, the Nigerian Financial Intelligence Unit (NFIU) issued guidelines preventing governors from interfering with statutory allocations accruing to local government councils from the federation account, according to a Guardian newspaper report.

Although the guidelines took effect since June 1, 2019, not much has changed in the local councils across the country. The state governors seem unwilling to comply with the guidelines, which of course, they rejected ab initio. However, in a recent statement, President Muhammadu Buhari, had warned all local government authorities not to give up their rights to their allocations released by the federal government. But until the autonomy of local governments is acknowledged and respected by these governors, the people at the grassroots will continue to suffer for lack of adequate funding.

Migration: Friend or Foe?

The two faced coin called migration means different things to different families. For some, it means increasing their pay checks and for others it means mortgaging the future of their loved ones just as it means taking care of their families for some others.

Many reasons abound why people choose to migrate irrespective of the situation or risks in their receiving country. These reasons include the need for quality education: the increasing escapades by insurgents have put the quality of education in Nigeria in doubts; the absence of employment opportunities: many graduates have no jobs and for this, the political and socioeconomic issues in Nigeria has continued to worsen making Nigerian youths ready to move whenever they have the opportunity thereby making many of them fall prey to traffickers.

What this means is that if the Nigerian economy does not improve soon or her government fails to act urgently, Nigerians will continue to migrate to other countries thereby making the human trafficking business easier and more lucrative for the perpetrators. The Nigerian government should, as a matter of urgency, address the problem of migration through job creation, creating a conducive environment for businesses to thrive and encouraging skilled labor so that those who already travelled abroad can return to help in national development.

With the increasing rate of insecurity in the nation, travelling outside the shores of the country is now the vogue hence the Nigeria youth is always in a hurry to leave. Oftentimes, irregularly or illegally. Little wonder migrants' remittances has surpassed both Foreign Direct Investment and Net Official Development Assistance inflows and is now considered one of the major inflows of foreign earnings to Nigeria that will help reduce poverty in households and have a positive impact on the economy but reverse is often the case as the rate of migration be it external or internal has a huge negative impact on the economy. When youths of a country are often on the look out for better life outside its shores, there is always lack of patriotism, disunity, unbelief in government to change situations, criminality, violence, and lack of manpower and infrastructural development. This is because output is low since production is now left in the hands of the weak and aged.

For instance in Nigeria the activities of Boko Haram forced many rural people to abandon their land and turned them into refugees even in their own country. Because of this, food production is low thereby, making food stuff become luxury in the country as only the rich can now afford three square meals a day. Though Nigeria's net migration rate fluctuated substantially in recent years, the net migration rate for Nigeria in 2020-0.31 migrants per thousand population. It may be said to have decreased through 1975–2020 period ending at-0.31 migrants per thousand population in 2020 but Nigeria continues to experience high internal and external migration due to the size of its population, economic climate, as well as its porous borders especially with the rate of illegal migration often unrecorded.

Nigeria youths make up the largest population of the growing flow of migrants from Africa to developed countries especially Europe and America. In 2016, over 20,000 involved in the Mediterranean Sea crossing were reported to be from Nigeria and from 2017 until late 2019, hundreds of Nigerian migrants were deported from various destinations including Italy, Libya and South Africa. These young people embark on very risky journeys across the globe, not minding the casualties which continue to increase on a daily basis. Legit. ng an online newspaper in an article, counted the hope to increase income, lack of career advancement opportunities in Nigeria, more job opportunities outside the country, better education quality and advancing the exposure of their children as the 5 major reasons people leave Nigeria. So, understanding these reasons for leaving the country is important if Nigeria hopes to stem the tide.

Another report said, most young people who migrated under irregular circumstances were motivated by three factors: economic reasons, family dynamics and social media. This is mostly true but unfortunately, their hope is often dashed after what they see is always far from what they were promised and many often wished they never left the country when they did but the country's poverty level keeps worsening the National Bureau of Statistics in its 2019 Poverty and inequality in Nigeria Report highlighted that 40 percent of the total population or almost 83 million Nigerians live below the county's poverty line of 137,430 naira per year.

This increase is one of reasons Nigerians leave the country in search of "greener pastures." That is: to find security, work and new ways of life in other countries.

A recent report launched by the United Nations Development Program (UNDP) on irregular migration after interviewing 1,970 migrants agreed that in spite of the dangers the majority of irregular migrants from Africa to Europe would still travel. It therefore called on nations to create more incentives for young people at home and expand legal pathways for migration. This is with the aim of making the home a place people do not want to leave as well as put programs that go beyond deterrence and punishments in place to discourage young people from irregular migration.

According to the UN Migration Agency (IOM), this year alone, more than 3,000 people have died or gone missing on migratory routes. The journey across international borders and into unfamiliar communities exposes migrants to a range of dangers: physical and sexual violence, exploitation, abduction, and extortion. Children are particularly vulnerable to these risks but yet, it does not deter migration.

In order to forestall irregular or illegal migration, it is imperative that governments put machinery in motion to mitigate the adverse drivers and structural factors that hinder people from building and maintaining sustainable livelihoods in their countries of origin, they should try to reduce the risks and vulnerabilities migrants face at different stages of migration by respecting, protecting and fulfilling their human rights and providing them with care and assistance. Governments should address the legitimate concerns of states and communities, while recognizing that societies are undergoing demographic, economic, social and environmental changes at different stages that may have implications for and result from migration and strive to create conducive conditions that enable all migrants to enrich the societies through their human, economic and social capacities, to therefore, facilitate their contributions to sustainable development at the local, national, regional and global levels.

Revamping the NYSC Scheme
for Better Productivity

The National Youth Service Corps (NYSC) is a one year compulsory program set up by the Nigerian government of General Yakubu Gowon to involve its graduates in nation building and the development of the country and offer them startup experience in their areas of study. This mandatory service program has been in existence since 1973 for University and Polytechnic graduates to take part for one year in the service of their fatherland. It is a known fact that for one to be eligible to participate in the compulsory one-year youth service, one must be a graduate and below the age of 30 upon graduation. Otherwise, they will be issued a Certificate of Exemption.

The NYSC was established for specific reasons which include inculcating discipline in Nigerian youths through a tradition of hard work, patriotism and loyal service to Nigeria in any situation they find themselves; to enable Nigerian youths acquire the spirit of self-reliance by encouraging them to develop skills for self-employment and to contribute to accelerating the growth of the national economy. Other reasons include developing common ties amongst Nigeria youths to promote national unity and integration, equitable distribution and effective utilization of the skills of members of the service corps to satisfy national needs among many other reasons.

But a school of thought opines the present formation of the National Youth Service Corps, NYSC, has failed the nation as it has been unable to contribute to national development which is one of the reasons for its establishment and has to be restructured to become a more result oriented program. It believes that every year, graduating youths from different schools in the country are subjected to assignments that have no yardsticks for measurement and often-times end up with no benefit to the nation.

It is expected that with the numerous technical and technological challenges in Nigeria, graduates of various fields in the country should use the one-year mandatory service to practice what they learnt in school to solve the country's problems but it is often not the case as some of them, end up in offices not related to their discipline. This school of thought says present day NYSC is more like a playground of fun that can be redesigned to become a project-oriented program that would move the country forward. Thereby, making it a hub for inventors, a producing country, and agricultural innovations will become the hallmark for development.

The NYSC scheme was originally meant to serve as a catalyst for sustainable development in Nigeria especially after the Nigeria civil war but may be said to have failed in many respects in accelerating the socio-economic development of Nigeria, if measured by Eight-Scale Perception Index.

Early work experiences are amongst the numerous factors that shape the identities of adolescents and young adults which also influence their career choices. Therefore, enlisting in the Youth Service Corps should be an avenue to improve on the theoretical aspects of one's training and make them more practical, use them to develop a sense of corporate existence and common destiny of the Nigeria people. It should be the desired hope of shaping participants' future course through boosting engagement in civically oriented activities and work.

It should be a great opportunity to develop in the Nigerian youths the attitudes of mind, acquired through shared experience and suitable training which will make them more amenable to mobilization in the national interest.

In essence, the emphasis should be on revisiting the objectives of the National Youth Service Scheme to utilize its entrant's expertise to meet the technological demands of the country and bring her at par with other developed countries of the world. It will also go a long way in enhancing the technological know-how of the citizens.

The noble ideals on which the NYSC was established have mainly not been achieved; indeed the hope of achieving them seem to be receding. Poor financing of the tertiary education system and its resultant poor quality products present the nation with graduates who are of little value vis-a-vis the hope that their skills, knowledge and worldview can be shared equitably throughout the federation. Secondly, the poor economy has rendered employers unable to take in and adequately cater for corps members; coupled with insecurity, most corps members stay back in their home states and so, cannot make the contributions envisaged by its founders. Nigerian politics, as of the present, fosters a spirit of alienation among the youth who as a consequence, cannot be expected to be patriotic and give quality and committed service to the nation. Patriotism is developed by faith in a nation which is able to secure and provide adequately for the welfare of citizens. Tribalism is probably the greatest hindrance to the achievement of the goals of the NYSC scheme. To have one's tribe deprecated and not be accepted far from home is the greatest morale killer. In spite of these setbacks, it would be absurd to advocate that the NYSC scheme be scrapped completely. However, it would be great if the government begins as soon as possible to initiate the processes for reforming the NYSC scheme for it to meet the contemporary expectations and challenges of the twenty-first century. The lack of opportunities while in the National Youth Service Corps has continued to limit the functioning of their capabilities in sectors of national development needs. Hence the dire need to rethink the current deployment strategy of the NYSC so that youth capabilities fit the national development narrative.

Basically, the success of the youth scheme depends on a national ethos which includes good governance in all ramifications: meritocracy, service delivery, transparency and accountability, free and fair elections, provision of adequate security for life and property etc. Without this and its products-stable and developing economic growth, faith in the nation, a community spirit of shared fate and values, peace and prosperity—the ideals of the youth service scheme will continue to flounder.

Digitalizing Vehicle and Driving
Licenses for Enhanced Security

With the new normal created by the coronavirus pandemic the world over, it has become increasingly necessary to make the vehicle and driver's licensing office more efficient in Nigeria. Though offices and agencies have been created at the federal and state levels for these purposes, actual issuance is often delayed as one registers in a state's licensing office but has to wait several months for the finished product since it has to come from the national offices of the Federal Road Safety Corps. What could be the reason? With computerization, issuance of licenses should be in minutes and hours not months. The banking institutions have achieved this feat as it can issue ATM cards in minutes and in a few hours, the cards are ready for use. This can be replicated in vehicle licensing.

Even though today, there are several agencies and bodies responsible for the issuance of vehicle and driver's licenses in Nigeria such as the Motor Vehicle Administration Agency (MVAA), the Federal Road Safety Corps, FRSC, and the Vehicle Inspection Service, VIO, the process of issuance of vehicle registration and licensing remains cumbersome and filled with quackery hence it cannot be used as a means of detecting or foiling crimes as is obtainable in more developed countries of the world. Looking at a brief history of motor vehicle administration in Nigeria, one is wont to ask "what has changed"? Before 1939, vehicle inspection was the duty of the Directorate of Works while motor licensing was carried out by the Motor Licensing Officer under the Federal Ministry of Finance. During the Second World War, officers from the Directorate of Works were drafted from Nigeria to serve in the colonial regiment of England for this, the Directorate of Works could no longer carry out the responsibilities of vehicle inspections. On 1st January, 1949, the Road Traffic Act to regulate and control vehicular traffic on the highways and the licensing of such vehicles and persons was promulgated by the colonial administration and this saw the Inspector General of Police being mandated to undertake the responsibilities of vehicle inspection as well as driver licensing and enforcement of the traffic rules regulations until 1958 when the constitution of Nigeria conferred the powers on regional governments to promulgate their own traffic laws. The regions however, adopted the existing laws so, the Inspector General of Police continued to serve as the Principal Licensing Officer until April, 1963 when the inspection units under Mechanical Departments of Ministry of Works of the regions were created by the Prime Minister through a majority vote and separate laws were made for each of the region that is: Northern Nigeria, Western and Eastern Nigeria respectively.

The coming into force of these laws and regulations ensured that drivers were properly tested before being issued with licenses and vehicles fully inspected and certified; and the Vehicle Inspection Officers (V.I.O.s) were properly conducting routine checks on all roads to ensure road safety. At the same time, collection of road tax as revenues were being paid promptly by defaulters. Though it could be said that the creation of states out of the then regions witnessed transferring of the functions to the states and later, the FCT, nothing much has changed only that all the agencies undertook the role of issuance. It would have been better if issuances are done in such a way that every car owner domiciled in a particular state, has a plate number of the state's issuing house and a driver's license of the said state to make it easier, faster and uniform. Such licenses must be digitalized so that when the citizen travels to another state or anywhere in the world, at the click of a button, the owner of a particular registered vehicle is known unlike what is obtainable today, where different states have different modes of registration. If this is the case, when a particular vehicle owner leaves his former state for another, he has the grace of 6months to effect changes on his licenses thereby, generating funds for government.

The benefits of a digitized licensing system cannot be over emphasized as they are enormous such as having the ability to help create a national database for the law enforcement agencies who, in turn, can use it for crime prevention and investigation and create cross relation between state agencies on information sharing especially as it relates to crime fighting. With a digitized licensing, national identification becomes unnecessary as the same agencies can also issue non driver's identification cards. Opening of bank accounts will also require such identification cards. The benefits cannot be quantified. There are so many benefits but the greatest of them all is that of security especially as it relates to fleet owners and drivers; in the event of theft, the plate can tell both the owner and law enforcement the location of the vehicle. The digital plates are engineered with tamper-resistant and anti-theft features.

Presently, digital number plates are in the Americas and hopefully it will get to Africa and Nigeria in particular. Though the price is said to be excessive for private consumers who want the technology, but digitalizing car registration is an innovative idea that can technically help to solve the problems of and help in the law enforcement of the motor vehicle department as well as help both the public and the vehicle users in a variety of ways.

The core idea is that each and every vehicle in the nation should have a unique digital identity which may be the same as that of the registered number of the car owner.

As in instituting changes in a democracy, these changes will require the actions of the National Assembly.

Reducing Road Transport Accidents in Nigeria

"My husband spoke to me on phone early that morning and said in a couple of hours he would be joining us here in Lagos, but now he's dead, we shall never see him again," cried a young mother of three whose husband James Okpara lost his life in a ghastly motor accident while traveling in a mass transit bus from Asaba to Lagos to visit his young family last year. The bus collided with a truck shortly before Ore, Ondo state, Nigeria. Okpara 52, died along with several others leaving behind a young heartbroken widow and three little children aged 15, 13 and 10. "Who will help me care for these children", queried the young mother with tears-filled eye.

Loss of a Bread Winner Brings Poverty and Sufferings Every time there is a fatal road accident, families of victims suffer in many ways. The loss of a family member, no doubt brings sadness and other emotional pains. Most bereaved indicate feelings of emptiness and frustration particularly in cultures where family bond is still strong. For someone who losses a spouse, the suddenness of the event can bring loneliness and hopelessness, and such situation has led many to their untimely deaths resulting to more sufferings for little children left behind. Authorities have however suggested that feelings of sadness, emptiness, loneliness, frustration and depression are not the only consequences that may arise from road mishaps.

The cost of Road Traffic Accidents (RTAS) certainly goes beyond emotional and psychological losses. The cost of accident to a family, community or nation may also include cost of treatment for injured and labour loss incurred as a result of injuries, or death of victims. Many analysts have estimated such labour loss to cost millions of dollars each year. The international Journal of physical sciences (2013) quotes a WHO estimate that puts global annual loss from injuries as high as 50 million dollars. Such annual loss is obviously enormous, especially for low and middle-income countries with high rate of RTAS who also rely on this productive population to help improve the national economy. Again, many in these countries depend on one, or a few family breadwinners, such as father and the eldest son (and in recent times the mother), to provide for the family needs. In rural communities, many family members have migrated to cities to find greener pastures and these help, not only to provide feeding supports but also help with funds for farm expenses, including farm land procurement, cultivation, seedling, weeding and pest control. "My family's bread winner is my elder brother who lives in Abuja", says Inusa, a student of Kaduna polythenic, Kaduna, Nigeria. "My brother provides for my education here and at the same time send money to our father in the village for farming purposes," Inusa asserted. Inusa's elder brother and James Okpara earlier mentioned above are just examples of hundreds of thousands of bread winners who daily cater for dependent family members.

A young female banker says the reason she remains unmarried is because her family depends on her for their livelihood. "I take care of my mother who is diabetic and my four younger siblings since I am the only one working in my family." Rebecca lost her father when she was 20 years old, and had assisted her mother care for their family until the mother became very ill. The question 'who will help care for the family?' is frequently repeated in many societies whenever a fatal road accident occurs leaving a bread winner dead or injured. Thousands of families have suffered untold economic hardship after losing their bread winners to fatal road accidents. Such sufferings do not stop with the poor. The rich also suffer. There are several instances of rich families that go bankrupt just few years after losing their bread winners. But poor or rich, there is increasing evidence that children, women and the aged are the worst hit in the family when fatal road accident occurs. This group suffers most from economic hardship when the bread winner is no longer around to care for them. In some cultures, women are restricted from economic activities, and are therefore incapable of fending for themselves and their little ones. The entire family often goes hungry with none to help.

Road Traffic Accident Figures on the High

"The incidence of fatal road accidents in Nigeria is phenomenal," reports vitus Nwankwo Ukorji, a research fellow at the French institute for research in Africa (IFRA – Nigeria), in a trend analysis of fatal road accidents covering the period June 2006 to May 2014. Ukorji, citing a Nigerian watch database, reports that "...15,090 lives were lost to fatal road accidents in 3,075 events. The highest fatality occurred in 2013 (2,061 deaths), a 2.8% increase from the 2012 record of 1,652 deaths. The result further notes that there had been 964 recorded deaths between January and May 2014 alone. Painting a more glooming picture, the reports states, "Nigeria is ranked second-highest in the rate of road accident among 193 countries of the world", continuing, the reports states, "aside from the Boko haram crises, accidents are currently by far the main cause of violent deaths in Nigeria." The WHO had also adjudged Nigeria the most dangerous country in Africa with 33.7 deaths per 100,000 population each year in a report that says one in every four road accident deaths in Africa occurs in Nigeria. Concluding the report, Ukorji in a rather bitter note reflects, "the WHO survey and the FRSC report of 5,693 fatal road accidents in 2009 leave no doubt about the dangerous situation in Nigeria records."

Why Do Road Traffic Accidents Occur?

To effectively tackle the problem of increasing road traffic accidents, more people need to understand why these unwanted accidents still occur. In the case of Nigeria, poor maintenance of existing road network has long been identified as a leading cause of road accidents in the country. This is closely followed by poor vehicle maintenance by vehicle owners and drivers making it difficult for early detection of faults and to forestall possible breakdown of vehicles which may become hazardous to other road users. However, aside from some environmental factors such as heavy rain fall and dust that may threaten driver's visibility and result in accidents, some experts agree that human factor accounts up to ninety percent of road accidents. These include driver fatigue where the driver gets tired and can suddenly fall asleep, poor sight, health failure, ignorance of traffic rules and signs, non-compliance, drug and alcohol abuse. Other causes of road accidents, according to these experts include many unsafe driving behaviors such as driving and drinking, smoking, pinging, making calls or sending text messages, selecting music or radio frequencies. The list also includes speeding, reckless driving and gross irresponsibility on the part of drivers.

But many commercial drivers have also accused passengers who sometimes cajole commercial drivers forcing them to go beyond acceptable speed limits to enable those passengers meet their appointments at the risk of all other persons in the vehicle. Yet, recklessness of drivers, particularly those of trailers, petroleum product tankers and other heavy duty trucks, has been blamed for the wanton waste of lives in most Nigerian roads. This has led Lagos State Government to introduce a new policy recently restricting the movement of this category of vehicles within Lagos metropolis. Early in September 2015 the National association of Nigerian Students (NANS) threatened to embark on a nationwide protest to protest to press home the demand for the banning of these trucks from plying major Nigerian highways between the hours of 0600 and 2100 many observers are however wondering, can the students achieve the feat?

What You Can Do to Prevent
Road Traffic Accidents

Good enough, following the United nations decision on May 11, 2011 to adopt the period 2019-2020 as the decade of Action for Road safety, Nigeria's Federal road Safety commission (FRSC) has put in place relevant programs to help prevent road accidents in the country. However this effort must be matched with proper program implementation. It is also very important for all levels of government in the country to muster the required political will to make the necessary investments in the sector, especially in road construction, maintenance and expansion.

Many have accused politicians of greedily diverting funds approved for such purposes into private accounts. This corrupt practice no doubt contributes to the violent deaths on the roads and endangers both the people and the Nigerian economy. Nevertheless, road users themselves need to take the responsibility of ensuring their own safety. Road users can make little efforts to see that everyone leaves home and gets back to the waiting arms of loved ones safe and sound. And to make this happen drivers need to do the right things all the time. Conducting regular checks and maintenance on the vehicle, observing traffic rules and road signs, obeying vehicle parking procedures, avoiding driving when on alcohol and drugs (some medications can make you drowsy and require that you do not drive) and when you feel tired or drowsy, learning to keep from driving are some of the needful.

Recklessness and other risky behaviors must be resisted either as a driver or passenger because of the precious lives you can help save by doing so. And remember road accident destroys not only people and their dreams, it impoverishes the family, Community and the nation alike.

The general rule is for everyone, drivers and passengers, to always think safety first. You can also talk to friends, colleagues and family members on the need to keep every journey safe every time.

Any Good Side of Coronavirus?

One day the world woke up to a new world order which has placed the year 2020 as one of the most phenomenal year in history. What, with the myriads of strange occurrences, chief of which is the Coronavirus global epidemic that has kept more than half the world population indoors for weeks on end on compulsory lockdown while continually going from house to house like a mad grim reaper, choking life out of multiple thousands of people. At last count, over 2 million persons have tested positive to the virus and over 161,000 deaths globally.

Many conspiracy theories have also been generated on the whys and wherefores of this pandemic. But this write-up is focused on highlighting if any, the good side of the lockdown necessitated by the virus.

Religious/Spiritual Purgation

Despite the varying conspiracy theories, one prediction everyone appears to agree with is that the world will never remain the same after this Coronavirus scare. One of the worst hit organizations by the virus is the religious organization. Religious organizations have always thrived on gathering of people which is against social distancing as a strategy to saving mankind from viral annihilation. So, with government's imposed lockdown and social distancing, religious physical meetings became illegal. This has given rise to a form of spiritual sanitization among the religious and their organization. The Catholic Church hierarchy introduced a spiritual form of observing their festivals. Families were seen holding solemn moments together, observing the Easter, the holy Communion spiritually. The experience has been sublime. Thanks to Coronavirus scare and the lockdown, the rat race has been checked and everyone is in recess and people now have time to engage in solemn reflections.

There has also been a separation between the wheat and the tares in the claims of many religious leaders. The social media is afire with criticisms of religious leaders who hitherto had been claiming to be healers of stubborn health conditions. From the Chris's to the Major/Senior Prophets, all have been challenged to intervene with their self-acclaimed spiritual powers and heal the ever increasing number of Corona virus victims. One would call to mind the frustration of one of the new generation religious leaders who was recorded as he screamed at Coronavirus; "Where do you come from? Where do you form? Who are you?" Hilarious as that may sound, it depicted the frustration among those who hitherto claimed to have supernatural healing powers and proved that when the chips are down, scientific solutions remain the most reliable in the human existential experience. And so, more people now attend to religious practices with fewer fundamentalisms and more humanism.

Healing Homes

This lockdown occasioned by the Corona virus scare has also served as a catalyst for diagnosing and, in more occasions, healing many homes in Nigeria. Couples who had before now become strangers to each other because of the 9 to 5 schedule of work have now been forced to spend time together and really get to know each other. The social media again revealed how many fathers who had been distant to their children have started bonding well with them. A lady was telling a radio presenter during a show how she was grateful for the lockdown which has kept her husband home attending to his duties as her husband and kept him away from late hour beer parlors. Social scientists have also noted that with the compulsory grounding of most couples, those dysfunctions which had hitherto been swept under the carpet are forced to surface to be dealt with conclusively so that relationships are thereby healed or dissolved as the case may be.

New Respect for the Mother of Economy

While traders and artisans groan over the lockdown and its attendant effects on the economy, farmers are unperturbed as they are self-sufficient. On the same radio program cited earlier, one caller said he was a farmer and that he was not affected by the lockdown as he had enough food in his store as well as his farm to keep him and his family through the period for any length of time the lockdown took though regretted that there will be a great loss after the lockdown as most of their produce are perishable and as such would have spoilt by the end of the lockdown. Another called to say that one of the lessons he has learnt was the dire need for every household to have a farm even if it is just a vegetable farm. The caller noted that the virus only consumed those whose immunity was compromised most times as a result of poor diet. "But if we all made fresh fruits and vegetables the main stay of our diet, we have nothing to fear; Corona Virus or not," he said. Also, thanks to Corona virus, essential services have been given their right of place above other services. Only persons who are certified providers of essential services are allowed to ply the roads amidst this location.

Emphasis on Good Hygiene

Another very prominent aspect of this Corona Virus scare is the emphasis it has made our society give to good hygiene culture. People now wash their hands as often as they should. Marketplaces, hospitals and homesteads now insist on washing and sanitizing of hands by visitors. People now take their baths more often and people are no longer pushed to keep their homes and surroundings, especially their toilets, clean. I marveled when I went to the village to visit some relations at the beginning of this lockdown and the first sight that caught my interest was a water dispenser, liquid soap and hand sanitizer sitting visibly by the gate and they laughingly insisted that I washed my hands thoroughly before entering or touching anyone. I complied because I was glad that such was becoming the culture even in villages and it is expected that things would remain so, long after the Corona virus era.

Call to Action/Conclusion

While the lockdown continues and an end is not yet in sight for the Corona virus, humanity is gradually adopting a more serene attitude to life and living. This is the time to take stock as an individual, change your attitude to life and think out of the box for that is the only way to survive in the new world order. As a government what have you learnt, what are those things that need to be changed or mended to give your citizens better and safer lives? What needs to be done and are you willing to do them? It is obvious that there is nothing completely evil or good in itself as the duality of things acts on all things. Instead of getting worked up over the bleak reality Corona virus epidemic has shown us, we should take solace in the fact that the epidemic came with some good aspects to change the world, our country and our families for the better. So, let's take advantage of this and make our world a better place for all irrespective of race, status, class, gender, tribe or religion.

Kidnapping Business in Nigeria

In the 1980s' Many Nigerians only watched Kidnapping on Hollywood movies. It was an act for entertainment that we never imagined could happen live in Nigeria. Then in late 1990s' the first few incidents were reported in the niger delta region where militants deployed it taking hostages of some foreign nationals to arm twist oil multinationals into negotiations. It was the beginning of a huge industry that kidnapping has become today. Indeed, kidnapping has grown into an embarrassing national security challenge that is currently gulping hundreds of millions of naira and many lives have been lost before ransom is paid. Kidnapping has unfortunately developed from targeting few foreigner experts to just any one in the country. Kings, governors, local government chairpersons, members of houses of assembly and their family members have been touched in recent years. No one seems safe anymore. And the situation becomes even ridiculous when security chiefs are not spared. Some years ago, a young man popularly called Evans, came to national prominence for the wrong reasons; he was arrested in Gbagada area of Lagos, from where he reportedly coordinated a huge kidnapping empire that took millions of naira from victims and their families in ransoms. Evans was revealed to source his victims from social media platforms. Kidnapping for money is certainly no longer the problem of the Niger Delta or Lagos state alone. It's not even restricted to South eastern states where the then Bakasi local vigilante fought to dismantle the illegitimate networks.

Today, the entire north central states of Benue, kogi, Kaduna, zamfara, katsina, seem to have been overtaken by these criminal elements. Kidnapping has not only become a huge money spinner, it has also become a national tragedy that's now taunting everyone, including the high and low.

Travelling on Nigeria's poorly managed highways is now a nightmare for many. Except for those who cannot afford the cost of flight tickets, the use of airplanes has become the easy way out for interstate travels. This of course mounts pressure on available local airplanes, making it more expensive than usual. Kidnapping in Nigeria today has gone far beyond kidnapping of the 2000s where Niger delta militants kidnapped for a few million naira. While criminal elements around the country are still getting themselves richer in millions of ransom payments for kidnapping for adult citizens and foreigners, Boko Haram and the so-called bandits operating in the North east and North west of Nigeria have raised the bar of ransom payments. School children are now the target of kidnapping by these ones.

Beginning in 2014 with the kidnapping of nearly 300 Chibok students in Borno state by Boko Haram terrorists and culminating in 2020 with the kidnapping of 344 students from another school in kastina state by bandits redefining the nature and term of engagement of kidnapping. According to a recent BBC report, "Kidnapping hundreds of students rather than road travelers, guarantees publicity and government involvement in negotiations, which could mean millions of dollar in ransom payments."

This suggest that North east and North west kidnapper elements have taken the stake higher by targeting school children, and getting governments to negotiate and possibly part with hundreds of millions as ransoms for their freedom.

Such development, even though has recorded relative success for release of school children may not augur well for the country on the long run because of the negative implications. Thankfully, the president has reportedly expressed similar reservation in ransom payments by state governments.

Meanwhile between January and February of 2021, about 1, 181 people including 362 children and 103 females were kidnapped in Nigeria, according to News Situation Tracking, an analytical report of WAMEP. These are not just statistics. These numbers involve real people who have had to endure both emotional and psychological trauma in the hands of criminals. Nigerians at home and abroad, young and aging, are standing up against the spate of kidnapping in the country, which is fast destroying our socio-economic activities.

The national government that is in control of both policing and the armed forces needs to stand up to its responsibility of protecting lives and properties across Nigeria. The present state of insecurity and rising cases of kidnap in the country are overwhelming and should not continue.

Both federal and state government in Nigeria must be held accountable for the lapse in our security architecture. It is, within the rights of all Nigerians to be protected for us all to live in peace.

Participatory Budgeting and Development in Nigeria

Successful political administration depends to a large extent on efficient and effective making and implementation of the budget. The budget is a tool for the implementation of social, political and economic policies and priorities which impact on the lives of the masses but often times, people in the helm of affairs negate this all important aspect of governance.

Though the legislative houses participate during the approval and audit stages, budgeting in Nigeria is seen as an exclusive preserve of the executive arm of government, especially as it concerns budget preparation and implementation.

This may well be why since 1999 when democratic rule returned in Nigeria, all efforts to ensure participatory governance have never received the support it deserved especially by the ruling class since they see it as a threat to their collective interest; thereby making opportunities for citizens, and participation in governance in Nigeria to remain limited. Indeed, exclusion from participation in the budgetary process is tantamount to a breach of the democratic process and political and economic marginalization are rooted in exclusion from the budget making process.

Nevertheless, a budget is the principal instrument of fiscal policy used to encourage stable growth, sustainable development and prosperity in the economy. It outlines what economic and non-economic activities a government wants to undertake with special focus on policies, objectives and strategies for accomplishments that are substantiated with revenue and expenditure-projections.

It is through a budget that the statement of expected income and expenditure of any government over a period, usually one year, are indicated therefore, budgetary allocation which means the amount of cash or budget allocated to each item of expenditure in the financial plan depends heavily on information, analysis and projections.

In spite of these information, analysis and projections, governments, Ministries, Departments and Agencies renegade on the budget made just to satisfy their personal desires For instance, a total of NGN640bn was distributed to the three tiers of government by the Federation Account Allocation Committee, FAAC, in February, 2021 as federation allocation for the month of January, 2021. of this amount, inclusive cost of collection to NCS, DPR and FIRS, federal government received N226.998bn, the states received N177.171bn while local governments got N131.399bn just as oil producing states received N26.777bn as derivation (13%of Mineral Revenue. All these monies notwithstanding, some states in Nigeria have nothing to show and many of them still owe workers' salaries.

It is expected that all those who get a share of the allocation should utilize it for what it was budgeted for but that is often not the case in Nigeria as many offices channel the monies into various uses other than what it was budgeted for at the detriment of the masses. This may well be the reason citizens are not carried along in budgeting.

What participatory budgeting is, should be or what it is not has always been a topic for discussion. While some school of thought argue that participatory budgeting is a process through which citizens can contribute to decision making over at least part of a governmental budget, another says it should be open to any citizen who wants to participate can do so, yet another believes it should combine direct and representative democracy, involve deliberation and not consultation, redistribute resources to get to the poor, and must be self-regulating, so that participants can help define the rules governing the process, including the criteria by which resources are allocated.

The problem of budget allocation in Nigeria has remained divisive over the years because the country is still divided between the minority ruling class, who controls both the economic and political power of the society, so, dominates and exploits the governed, and the dominated and exploited working class, who have neither economic nor political power, but are in the majority yet powerless. The states therefore, mainly functions as an instrument of class domination, with which the ruling class protects itself and exploits the working class. A Dr. Uche Igwe led study on illicit financial flows advocates that to secure best value in terms of allocation and utilization scarce resources in Nigeria, the concept of value Money Audit, due process and cost Audit must be adhered to strictly and if properly applied alongside good public procurement philosophy will engender a strong legal, organizational and professional framework to make budgeting and budget implementation in the Nigerian Public Sector robust and effective. Oftentimes, stories of disparity between budget and its implementation in Nigeria's public sector make the headlines in newspapers, priority in public discourses and academic journals and they all come back with the same answers-corruption, fluctuating oil revenue, unstable economic parameters and poor budget monitoring.

It therefore, becomes imperative that there's professionalism in post project review technique of value for money concept, performance measurement and benchmarking so that the continuous process and improvement recorded can be imbibed as a national corporate culture.

It is disheartening that in spite of the specific appropriate laws, the commitment phase of the expenditure process is a fertile ground for corrupt activities because most times, there is partial or total disregard of procurement regulations and procedures, even where they exist.

There are several constraints to budget implementation, an example being corruption which always hinders budget implementation. Ministries often have no adequate measures to address budget variances, they do not adequately monitor budget so as to achieve the expected goal.

Poor and unrealistic policy implementation has been the bane of socio-economic development in developing countries like Nigeria as budget implementation is not just about executing the approved budget. In many countries of the world, the implemented budget varies from the adopted one this could be as a result of the country's fiscal conditions, stability and certainty in the country's finances, the role of the finance ministry, and the type of budget system. A highly itemized budget may experience more variance than the budget which gives managers spending discretion.

Giving spending units more flexibility in implementing their budgets, is now the trend in contemporary public management even though this may not be appropriate in countries with inadequate management controls.

Appropriate implementation, leads to development which integrates people into the plans and policies of government who in turn, provide services of importance to its citizens in rural and urban areas such as provision of basic services like water, roads, health facilities, education. Unfortunately, in the states for instance, the role of government in providing these services has attracted public concern as a result of increasing rate of poverty among the rural people. Some scholars associate this development to poor budgeting and implementation while others blame the federal government for interference. Whatever the case may be, there is dire need to liberate the people from untold hardship.

The foregoing clearly shows that the budget is in essence, a political tool in which a people's aspirations and strategies for progress and inclusion in a nation's body politic are embedded. A representative of the people must therefore not only be a reliable and empathetic connoisseur of these aspirations and needs but also be knowledgeable, astute and charismatic enough to get them into the budget and monitor their successful implementation.

A representative of the people must have an intensive knowledge of how population density, derivation from crude oil, ecological situations, zoning and other situations that affect the lives of the people play in the preparation and implementation of the national budget. In that way, he or she will be in a position to effectively represent the people's interests.

Ranching for National Prosperity in Nigeria

The Governors of Southern Nigeria met in Lagos on July 5, 2021, for a review of the security situation and other issues confronting the country, after which it was resolved "That Wednesday, 1 September 2021 shall be set aside for the promulgation of the anti-open grazing law in all member States."

This resolution stemmed from increasing herders/farmers clashes and the herders insistence on open grazing. As at 2019, the NGO, Mercy Corps, in its report estimates that cattle herders/farmers clashes in Nigeria has claimed more than 7, 000 lives over the previous five years costing the economy$13 billion annually.

Over the years, demand for beef in the country of about 200 million people had been met primarily by Fulani pastoralists who follow the age-long tradition of raising and driving cattle down south for pasture before selling them, which has led to frequent clashes with local farmers.

Today with much reported death and huge loss to the economy, resulting from these conflicts, more people are advocating for ranching as a viable solution. But herders seem to cling to the long tradition of open grazing with reports of illegal deployment of arms, such as AK-47 for protection of their lives and cattle from possible attacks.

Yet there's frequent report of encroachment and destruction of crops and farmlands by herders, keeping these conflicts unabated. A Vanguard report notes that: "The friction has roots dating back more than a century. Drought, population growth, the expansion of sedentary farming into communal areas but also poor governance has played a role." Such neglect has herders feeling isolated, according to Ibrahim Abdullahi, Secretary of GAFDAN, a national union of herders. Abdullahi told the Vanguard:" Nothing was done to implement the grazing reserves designed by the law in the 1960. Most of the land have been sold and now cultivated by farmers who grow crops."

But many commentators insist that time has changed, and the business of cattle rearing ought to be modernized as is the case with other important beef and milk producers around the world. Questions have been asked about the individual owners behind the cattle business in Nigeria.

Why is it difficult for these individuals to adopt ranching and make substantial investments to boost productivity, minimize the risk of loss of cattle and possibly eradicate these associated conflicts? Again, why must Nigeria continue to lose thousand of lives and billions of dollars in herders/ farmers conflicts when it is one of the least countries in beef and milk production globally?

Let us look at the following statistics from available data. Nigeria, with a population of 200 million, has beef consumption of between 360, 000 and 380, 000 tons and projected to grow up to 1.3 million tons by 2050, according to experts. Yet, a world cattle inventory in 2020 published in April 16, 2021 by Rob Cook of Farmcentric, ranking countries with the most cattle states that: "India had the largest cattle inventory in the world in 2021 followed by Brazil and China....India's cattle's inventory was reported at 305.5 million head in 2021, accounting for roughly 30 percent of the world's inventory."

According to this report, India, Brazil and China accounted for roughly 65 percent of the world's cattle inventory in 2021.

Following is the global ranking of countries with the most cattle for 2021:

1. India-305, 500, 000
2. Brazil-252, 700, 000
3. China-95, 620, 000
4. USA.–93, 595, 000
5. EU.-.85, 545, 000
6. Argentina-53, 831, 000
7. Australia-23, 217, 000
8. Russia 17, 953, 000
9. Mexico-17, 000, 000
10. Uruguay 11, 946, 000
11. Canada-11, 150, 000
12. New Z.-10, 063, 000
13. Egypt.-7, 850, 000
14. Belarus.-4, 300, 000
15. Japan-. 3, 922, 000
16. S. Korea-. 3, 774, 000
17. Ukraine-. 3, 001, 000

Although previously quoted Vanguard newspaper report estimates Nigeria's cattle population at 20 million, this fact is clearly not represented in the above table provided by FAS/ USDA (head), suggesting Nigeria might not be in the league of serious global players.

The RUGA project promoted by the federal government to solve the herders/farmers conflicts was resisted by many, but private investors can be encouraged and supported to make meaningful investment to generate returns for stakeholders from meat and milk production.

Ranching remains the viable pathway to improved productivity in the business of cattle farming for individual and national prosperity.

Quest for State Policing in Nigeria

The 1979 Constitution of the federal republic of Nigeria gave Nigeria Police Force the sole jurisdiction to enforce internal security all over the states of the federation including the federal capital territory.

This gigantic organization has been managed and controlled by the federal government even though a state governor is regarded as chief security of the state with enabling security vote in the state's annual budget.

But in more recent years, the clamor for stateowned police has increased throughout the country. Observers have linked this development to the heightened insecurity in Nigeria.

Okemuyiwa Akeem Adedeji Ph. D, thinks the popularity of state Policing has increased due to the surge in the rate of sophisticated crimes being perpetrated across the country and the apparent inability of the federal police command to contain the challenges.

Indeed, there have been several conflicting voices with genuine concerns in this debate either for or against state policing.

One such writer who expressed the view of supporters had written that "it is believed that the closeness of the state police to the society of its jurisdiction places it in more proactive position for the detecting and uprooting of any emerging crime before it grows."

Another argument against a centralized police force is its size and complex weave of network, which commentators believe need to be pruned.

The Nigeria Police Force has grown in manpower from meagre 12,000 in 1960 to about 400,000 today.

Some other supporters of state policing point to state's ability to fund policing in their areas. One good example is that of Ex-Governor Rauf Aregbesola. While in office as governor of Osun state in 2014, he was able to chase out criminal elements and enforce the peace in the state by purchasing and donating to Nigeria Police Force, a helicopter for aerial surveillance, and 25 more superior Armoured Personnel Carriers (APC).

Since then though, many states have provided security logistics for NPF, indicating their financial ability for state policing.

Yet, those opposed to state policing fear that state governors could turn the police to their instrument of oppression, or to private armies. This fear of course, is not unfounded considering the role of the police under Hassan Katsina in July 1966, and under Sam Akintola in 1964.

But since creation of the force, NPF, like others in colonised Africa has served the interest of the ruling class. Okechukwu Nwanguma of NoPrin, a nonprofit organization committed to police reform in Nigeria claims "The Nigeria Police Force…was set up by the British to cater to the whims of the ruling class and that explains why despite Nigerians being in charge since 1964, policing in Nigeria has not improved."

A 2004 report in the Police Journal also highlighted similar sentiment about the Nigerian Police, stating that the police still operate "with the same arbitrariness, ruthlessness, brutality, vandalism, incivility, low accountability to the public and corruption," as it did in colonial times.

Candidly, the same conclusions can be reached by any vigilant observer with the long list of victims of extra judicial killings and brutality. One recent article by Godwin Aniagbo, titled Nigeria's Police: The lingering effects of a colonial massacre, and published by British Broadcasting Corporation, puts it succinctly, "Complaints about brutal policing in Nigeria today echo the reaction to the shooting dead by colonial policemen of striking coal miners in 1949."

So Nigeria Police Force today, as it's presently constitutes, is still much the same way its colonial creators left it, and a major problem with it is behavioral rooted in wrong perception of role and poor orientation. This also means that unconstitutional use of the police force could be carried out by anyone that controls it, federal or state.

Therefore, to douse the persisting fears of those against state policing, the debate should not stop at whether or not, but must include a conversation on the How's.

For instance, the constitution must be clear on how state policing can be operated in the country without serving as a ready tool in the hands of desperate politicians.

How Independent is Nigeria's Judiciary?

The Judiciary is the third arm of government that interprets, defends and applies the law to the facts of each case, according to Wikipedia.

It's thought that for the Judiciary to fulfill its sacred roles within the state, there should be powers and protection given to it; and such powers as contained in the Nigerian constitution provide for the Judiciary to stand separate and free from interferences and influences of other arms of government as well as other partisan interests.

Wikipedia explains that "Judicial Independence serves as a safeguard for the rights and privileges provided by a limited constitution and prevents executive and legislative encroachment upon those rights. It serves as a foundation for the rule of law and democracy......under an independent judicial system, the courts and their officers are free from inappropriate intervention in the judicial affairs. With this independence, the Judiciary can safeguard people's rights and freedoms which ensure equal protection for all."

The independence of the Judiciary enabling the making of fair decisions will ultimately determine the effectiveness of the law and how the people view the government and its laws.

This also applies to economic and diplomatic stakeholders within the international community.

There's no doubt Nigeria has made progress to reinforce the judicial independence through constitutional provisions and by other means. Section 6 of the 1999 Nigerian Constitution clearly vests judicial powers of the federation in the courts. Section 4 (8) of that constitution in the effort to further safeguard the Judiciary also provides for the power of judicial scrutiny to avoid enactment of laws that seek to oust the jurisdiction of court. Section 17 (1) (e) of the constitution also provides that: "The independence, impartiality and integrity of Courts of Law, and easy accessibility there to shall be secured and maintained," although this provision may not bite by the virtue of Section 6 (6) (c) of the constitution.

Furthermore, the Federal Government of Nigeria established the National Judicial Council (NJC) in accordance with the provisions of Section 153 of the 1999 Constitution as amended 'to protect the Judiciary of Nigeria from the whims and caprices of the Executive.' Statutory duties of this council, according to the official website include several judicial functions such as advising the President of Nigeria and Governors on issues related to the Judiciary.

They also perform disciplinary functions as well as appointment and nomination of executive members of the Judiciary. In these we see the efforts of Nigerian government to reinforce and protect the independence of Judiciary, but critics insist there's no such thing in reality.

These contrasting voices particularly from members of Judiciary themselves cast the question mark on how those aforementioned provisions have been implemented.

A Port Harcourt based lawyer, Mr. Festus Oguche, in an interview with Bridget Chiedu Onochie of Guardian newspaper, while finding questions on judicial independence declared, "We have gotten to a point in our national life that we must shun politics and address issues as they are.

There is no talk about judicial independence in our country in the midst of all the challenges and upheavals the system has been subjected to over the years. It is just not there. Suffice it to mention that the mere existence of the judicature as an arm of government under a doctrinaire constitutional power separation arrangement, does not give any guarantee of independence or autonomy to a system beyond the constitutional pronouncement."

Although agreeing to some visible innovations and advancements in the country's constitutional development, Mr Oguche insisted, I agree that there has been gains and innovations here and there in the system… particularly in the areas of charging judicial funds to the consolidated revenue fund, the establishment of the National Judicial Council, the hierarchical organization of the courts, the judicial code and the criteria for appointment of judicial officers, but the independence or autonomy of the system as we can now see from its functional perspective remains merely cosmetic. Truth is that the loopholes created by the constitution that engender extraneous interference particularly from the executive and political elites hold sway."

Oguche, further claimed the presence of a 'a clear invasion of judicial sanctity and desecration of its hallowed integrity by political elites and state actors by the hounding and arrest of judges and the manner of their treatments in circumstances that even the National Judicial Council was helpless."

The issues of funding for the Judiciary, appointments and discipline which are crucial for effective judicial system, are some of the areas the so-called political class have apparently taken advantage of.

The replacement of Justice Walter Onnoghen, the former Chief Justice of Nigeria, described by Oguche as the highest point of executive interference and maneuver in the judicial system appears to give credence to these views of opponents. But there exist a good number positive steps taken by successive governments toward ensuring judicial independence in Nigeria, which many critics have so acknowledged. So what do we conclude, is Nigeria's Judiciary independent or not?

Towards National Peace and Cohesion

Sixty years after Nigeria gained her independence on October 1, 1960, the country taunted as Africa's most populous, and one of the most endowed nations of the world, is still enmeshed in a series of battles against ethnic, religious and criminal upheavals that have combined to undermine the country's national security, leading to many deaths and mass displacement of persons, children and women inclusive.

There's hardly a day without the news of bloody attacks, or kidnapping of citizens in one part of the country or the other.

There are secessionist elements in many parts of Nigeria calling for dismantling of the federation, and threatening the peace and cohesion, which the country has labored to earn since after the bloody civil war that ended in 1970.

Peace has become illusive with the federal and state governments engaging in what seems to be a wild goose chase.

Investigation shows that this widespread conflict and violence in Nigeria is rooted in war – time divisive propaganda and the continuing emphasis on ethnic and religious differences of Nigerians.

There are also issues of large scale poverty, inequality, inequity, injustice, marginalisation, unemployment and corruption that are serving the obnoxious interest of enemies of the state.

The first crucial step taken by the federal government of Nigeria to advance peace and cohesion after the civil war was the establishment of the National Youth Service Corps scheme by decree No. 24 of 22nd May 1973, which has now been repealed and replaced by decree 51 of 16th June 1993.

According to an official record, "The purpose of the scheme is primarily to inculcate in Nigerian youths the spirit of selfless service to the community, and to emphasize the spirit of oneness and brotherhood of all Nigerians, irrespective of cultural or social background.

The history of our country since independence has clearly indicated the need for unity amongst all our people, and demonstrated the fact that no cultural or geographical entity can exist in isolation."

Since the creation of the NYSC scheme, millions of Nigerian youths have successfully concluded their part, and many are now amongst Nigerian political elites.

Is the scheme achieving its most important goal of national cohesion 48 years after?

The International Dialogue on Peace building and State building (IDPS), an international organization for policy dialogue on peace building and state building, believes national cohesion to be "an instrumental pillar of conflict prevention, peace building and state building."

National cohesion is fundamental to building national peace, and helps engender sustainable national development.

It's therefore imperative to march the letters of any relevant policy designed to enhance national cohesion with necessary actions.

Even though the federal and state governments have made significant efforts to design and establish systems and programs to advance national peace and cohesion in Nigeria, which include the aforementioned National Youth Service Corps scheme, National Orientation Agency, Federal and state media agencies, among others, it is doubtful if the mandates of all these are being pursued and realised with equal zeal on both the governments and their handlers.

For instance, the National Orientation Agency was established by decree 100 of 1993 "to consistently raise awareness, positively change attitudes, values and behaviors, accurately and adequately inform; and sufficiently mobilise citizens to act in ways that promote peace and harmony among other things. NOA maintains over 5, 000 staff across the 36 states of the federation including Federal Capital Territory and the 774 local government offices. On it's official website, the NOA proudly proclaims that " No other organ of government has this kind of spread and capacity for public enlightenment and sensitisation campaigns."

But with all its huge structure and reach, how has the NOA helped to influence an average Nigerian?

Random phone conversation with some staff who pleaded anonymity revealed that poor funding from government is the basic challenge of this organization that should be a chief actor in the collective search for national peace and cohesion.

But NOA unfortunately remains on the sidelines as an inactive spectator. The United Nations Children Fund (Unicef), has warned that during conflicts in any part of the world, children suffer most, "children have always been the first victims of war.

Worldwide, armed conflict and other violence have upended the lives of hundreds of millions of children, leaving them displaced, under-nourished, out of school and at severe risk of exploitation and abuses."

The UN agency says while claiming that nearly 1 in 5 children today live in settings affected by armed conflict and war.

Indeed, the continuing absence of peace in any nation destabilizes the systems within it, and puts children and women mostly at risk of sundry abuses and premature deaths as we have recorded in some parts of Nigeria in recent years. In some states, schools have been closed down and suffering has multiplied in many homes. Ultimately, the search for national peace and cohesion in the country needs to engage the political will of people in government to ensure Justice, equity, fairness in governance and to provide all necessary supports required. Relevant government agencies must fully commit to fulfilling their mandates as spelt out by enabling laws.

Local Government Elections in Nigeria

Local government elections in Nigeria began 1987 under the Babangida Administration. It was the first time local government chairmen were elected through universal adult suffrage in the country.

According to Chinwe Nwanna in the Governance and Local Government Elections in Nigeria's Fourth Republic, following those first Elections "there were local government Elections in 1996, 1997 and 1998, but all proved problematic.

In 2003, local government Elections were postponed against the provisions of the constitution. Some States conducted local government elections in 2007, which were marred by violence, fraud and rigging; while some, like Lagos and Jos conducted theirs in 2008.

Others, like Anambra State, did not have local government elections until January 2014." This particular state Nwanna noted, had been ruled for many years by four successive governors-Chris Ngige, Peter Obi, Andy Uba and Virginia Etiaba and again Peter Obi without local council chairmen.

They appointed Caretaker Committees to run the affairs of the local governments in the state.

The story of local government elections in Nigeria since their creation, has been very disappointing and unprogressive. More recent experiences have also not changed the paradigm of the local government elections.

It does appear that this important election is being compromised and is fast losing its relevance.

In a Channels Television program, Politics Today, the Akwa Ibom state Residential Electoral Commissioner, Mr Mike Igini, described local government elections in Nigeria as organized crime. "Don't call them local government elections; they are nothing but organized crime or coronation ceremonies carried out across the Federal Republic of Nigeria.

But Nigerians are not doing anything about it; and you have lost your local governments because there is no democracy taking place there." On electoral violence, Igini stated "The political elites are the greatest threat to our democracy. Look at what happened in Akwa Ibom in 2019, look at all the properties that were destroyed. Eleven vehicles were set ablaze and 15 vandalized on the premises of INEC."

Also commenting on the last local government elections in Lagos State held on Saturday, July 24, 2021, a civil society organization that monitored the elections in Las, YIAGA Africa, observed that "Lagos State LGAs elections were characterized by similar shortcomings observed in other elections in Nigeria.

These include late opening of polls and deployment of election materials, disregard for the Electoral guidelines, confusion over the non-inclusion of a contesting party on the ballot, nondeployment of political party agents and voter apathy. "The organization also declared in its preliminary report on the Lagos poll that "Voter participation in these elections is abysmally low as citizens showed lack of interest in the process. This presents a disturbing trend in a state like Lagos with 6, 570, 291 registered voters and poses a major challenge to the practice of democracy in the state and Nigeria. With the level of turnout in the LGA elections, governance at the local levels in the state for the next four years will be by individuals who are elected by a very small fraction of the voting population."

Indeed across Nigeria, it has become a continuing display of impunity and electoral fraud orchestrated by the political elites.

The constant deployment of violent attacks at the polls, disregard for the electoral guidelines, ballot stuffing, ballot snatching and manipulation of vote figures are all directed at producing 100 percent win for predetermined candidates.

No wonder the increase in voter apathy recorded in nearly all parts where elections still hold. In some states, local governments are run by either Transition Committees or Caretaker Committees.

This trend is undoubtedly undemocratic, and often foist incompetent leadership on the people at the grassroots denying them of preferred candidates. The local government is the third tier of government in Nigeria, and have a very crucial role to play in extending governance and development to people at the grassroots. It remains a crucial partner for the provision and rehabilitation of rural infrastructures such as roads, primary healthcare, primary education, among others. It is the last hope of ordinary Nigerians.

The 1999 Constitution of the Federal Republic of Nigeria, as amended, guarantees a system of governance by a democratically elected council at the local government level. But the same constitution requires all states to enact laws for the establishment, structure, composition, finance and functions of local government councils.

The State Independent Electoral Commission (SIEC), is the instrument for the conduct of local government elections in all 36 states and the Federal Capital Territory. But state governments determine the tenure of elected local council officials, as well as when elections are conducted.

In this regard, the immense powers of state governments and their State Independent Electoral Commissions over the local governments cannot guarantee a free and fair Electoral process at the grassroots. This is why some political commentators have called on the Independent National Electoral Commission (INEC), to take up the responsibility of conducting local government elections. According to a former Ogun State People's Democratic Party (PDP) governorship aspirant, Oladipupo Adebutu, who is also a former member of the House of Representatives, "When we fail at the grassroots, everything else fails. The only solution to local government administration is to take away the election from states and allow credible elections where people can genuinely choose their leaders to exercise their franchise." Adebutu spoke at the second edition of the Ladi Adebutu Good Governance Symposium, held in Abeokuta.

Whatever solution agreed upon to reduce, or eliminate the overwhelming influence of state governments over the local governments, actions need to be taken quickly. The quality of local government elections has decisive implications on the quality of governance, and if we hope for even-spread of development for the people at the grassroots, then required changes must begin inernest.

High Cost of Governance in Nigeria

Early in 2020, Nigerians were awaken with the news of the approval to secure N35 million worth of Camry 2020 model for National Assembly members. The public outcry generated by what many Nigerians regarded as 'frivolous expenses' was loud, and once again, provoked the often asked question about bogus cost of governance Nigeria.

The purchase of such luxury for the 469 members (109 senators and 360 representatives), seems irreconcilable in a country with most its citizens wallowing in abject poverty. But most NASS members do not seem to agree.

However, the high cost of governance in the country has become a regular part of the national conversation in the public space for many years.

But each time, no progress has been made by successive governments to prune it down to realistic level. Instead, there has been continuous increase in allocations, which include salaries, allowances and other perks.

Sanusi Lamido Sanusi, Former Central Bank of Nigeria Governor, reportedly claimed that "70 percent of government revenue is spent on government itself." Such claim may have been validated by the 2021 National budget themed "Budget of Economic Recovery and Resilience", where total budget amounts to N13.6 trillion after the National Assembly added N505 billion to the proposed N13.08 trillion.

According to QueenEsther Iroanusi's report in Premium Times of December 31, 2020: "The legislature had approved a budget of N13.6 trillion against the N13.08 trillion proposed by the President.

Over N505 billion was added to the proposal and about a quarter of the budget will be funded by loans, indicating the income challenges the government faces."

It is sensible for Nigerians to expect prudence in the implementation of a loan-funded budget. But interestingly, the Premium Times added that "A total of N134 billion was budgeted for the National Assembly for 2021 out of the N496 billion allocated for statutory transfers.

"About N6 billion was added to the N128 billion proposed by President Buhari.

This is also despite the fact that the President had initially increased the National Assembly's budget from N125 billion in previous years to N128 billion for 2021." The report further stated that, "Until 2015, the annual allocations to the National Assembly had been N150 billion and between 2015 till date, the budget has been between N125 billion and now N134 billion."

But the issue of high cost of governance is not limited to bogus allocations from statutory transfers, or the National Assembly, it cuts across all organs of government, and extends from Federal government to State governments throughout Nigeria.

It also involves imprudent recurrent and capital expenditures. Many analysts have pointed to corruption in public sector as the chief driver of heightened cost of governance in the country. The civil servants and contractors have been accused for aiding politicians by providing the needed pipelines for outflow of diverted funds. "It is common that audit reports in Nigeria, at all levels, reveal flagrant disregard to rules and procedures, overthrow of financial discipline, accountability, probity and transparency, which the treasuries we're set up to establish and protect. These abuses/ breaches range from varied duplication of contracts, overvaluation of contracts, fictitious payments of contracts, non-certification of payment vouchers by the internal auditor, among others.

Other fraud in treasury activities may include over payment of existing staff, payment of salaries and allowances to dead or retired staff and ghost workers." (Agu, Osmond Chigozie: 2013).

Financial crimes involving public officers is currently engaging the attention of the Economic and Financial Crime Commission (EFCC), under the Buhari Administration, in an effort to curtail the excesses of public office holders and civil servants.

In a recent development, some officials of the River State Government were declared wanted by EFCC for criminal conspiracy, money laundering, misappropriation of public funds and abuse of office. In May 2021, Premium Times newspaper reported that, "In July last year, the Economic and Financial Crimes Commission arraigned three political office holders in Taraba State on six counts of conspiracy, criminal breach of trust, over their alleged role in the illegal withdrawal of N21 billion from the state coffers." Although as at press time, Bala Abu, Governor Darius Ishaku's media aide denied knowledge of the arrest.

The cable news of April 23, 2018, reported that the Economic and Financial Crimes Commission has arrested three high ranking People Democratic Party (PDP) senators on the list of alleged looters released by the federal government. The list of public office holders and civil servants across the country over fraudulent activities has been on increase in successive Administrations till this day under the Buhari Administration.

Corruption seems to be Nigeria's biggest developmental challenge, and an honest effort to bring it to the barest minimum would be the enduring legacy of any government.

Minimum level of corruption, probity, prudence and financial discipline can combine to become a powerful force required to establish and maintain reasonable cost of governance for the country.

Building the Integrity of INEC

Elections in colonial times were regulated and administered by regional laws and government until 1958 when the Electoral Commission of Nigeria ECN) was inaugurated to conduct the 1959 federal elections.

ECN was headed by a Briton, Ronald Edward Wraith and four regional representatives for east, west, north and Lagos.

In 1960, the Federal Electoral Commission (FEC), was established to conduct the first post-independence federal and regional elections that took place in 1964 and 1965. FEC was, however, dissolved following the 1966 military coup.

When peace returned to the country after the Nigeria civil war, the Federal Electoral Commission (FEDECO) was constituted in 1978 by the General Olusegun Obasanjo regime, which conducted the 1979 and the 1983 general elections.

After years of military encroachment, the General Abdulsalam Abubakar regime established the Independent National Electoral Commission (INEC), in 1998 to conduct the elections that ushered in the Nigerian Fourth Republic headed by Justice Ephraim Akpata

Since May 29, 1999, when INEC organized its first elections, several other elections have been held in Nigeria under different chairmen.

The list includes Justice Ephraim Akpata (1999), Abel Guobadia (2003), Maurice Iwu (2007), Attahiru Muhammadu Jega (2011), Amina Bala-Zakari (2015) and Mahmood Yakubu (2019).

But with more than two decades of experimentation, the INEC has suffered more controversies, which has largely impacted negatively on its public image with increasing erosion of public trust; In its ability to conduct free and fair elections in the country. Yet, Justice Uwais–led Electoral Reform Committee had declared that "free and fair elections are the corner stone of every democracy and the primary mechanism for exercising the principle of sovereignty of the people, and are, therefore, a crucial requirement for good governance in any democracy."

Indeed, the corporate mission of INEC is in sync with these fundamentals.

INEC was established by the 1999 Constitution of the Federal Republic of Nigeria to serve as an independent efficient Electoral Management Body (EMB) committed to the conduct of free, fair and credible elections for sustainable democracy in Nigeria.

No doubt, INEC has a huge role to play to strengthen Nigeria's nascent democracy, and this it must be seen to fulfill as the institution constitutionally empowered to ensure credibility and integrity of the election process.

Since the INEC derives its existence and authority from the

same constitution that acknowledges the sovereignty of the people, and their rights to select their preferred representatives in free and fair elections, it is in order to hold INEC accountable for its actions and inactions.

INEC remains the life wire of Nigeria's democratic process, and needs to recognize and take its stand as an unbiased umpire, and not yielding to any political force.

In the past elections, there have been several allegations against the electoral administrator, including widespread irregularities, such as ballot paper unavailability, large cancellation of valid votes, smart card-reader malfunctioning and others.

A review of past elections by Emmanuel Remi Aiyede, University of Ibadan, published in May, 2021, stated concerning the challenges of 2019 Elections. "My review of election observers' reports on the 2019 elections shows there were interferences with results collation by political party agents and security agencies with the connivance of electoral commission officials.

Inefficiencies in its operations manifested in puzzling discrepancies in records, voters' register data and declared election results.

Figures on the total number of registered voters announced before the election and the figures announced by electoral commission during the collation in 30 of the 36 states were inconsistent. Furthermore, poor logistics and supply of materials resulted in delays and created room for malpractices."

The sordid picture painted in this review is similar to those that emerged from other elections in the past. Allegations of partisanship and compromises have long trailed Nigeria's electoral management bodies, including INEC, and many factors have been identified for this.

Ahead of the coming 2023 elections, it is crucial to confront the issues and challenges that weaken the institution. Some very important reforms and amendments to the electoral acts need to be implemented to ensure true independence of the electoral body.

Critical among these recommendations made by the electoral

reform committee headed by Justice Uwais, include "removing the President's power to appoint the chairman and members of the commission, and making appointments the responsibility of the National Judicial Council.

The other vital issue is the change in the funding model for the commission to ensure it stays financially independent. These and many other aspects of the Uwais committee recommendations need to be vigorously pursued in order to build a stronger electoral institution that can guarantee integrity.

Nigeria and the Rule of Law

The rule of law, according to the Oxford English Dictionary, is described as "the authority and influence of law in society, especially when viewed as a constraint on individual and institutional behavior, (hence) the principle whereby all members of a society (including those in government) are considered equally subject to publicly disclosed legal codes and processes."

For further clarification, the United Nations employs the following definition: "The term rule of law refers to a principle of governance in which all persons, institutions and entities, public and private, including the state itself, are accountable to laws that are publicly promulgated, equally enforced and independently adjudicated, and which are consistent with international human rights, norms and standards.

It requires, as well, measures to ensure adherence to the principles of supremacy of law, equality before the law, accountability to the law, fairness in the application of the law, separation of powers, participation in decision-making, legal certainty, avoidance of arbitrariness and procedural and legal transparency."

While both definitions acknowledge and proclaim the supremacy or reign of the law over all individuals and institutions, without exemptions, the United Nation (UN) employs a definition that highlights important principles without which the term rule of law cannot be complete, and therefore, will not be applied.

These principles require that a law must be publicly promulgated, equally enforced and independently adjudicated, showing unambiguity, fairness, equality and transparency.

The law is also required to align with international human rights norms and standards for it to demand accountability from everyone, including the state itself.

For example, the rule of law requires that every Nigeria is considered equal and equally subject to the laws that have been made public and duly passed into law by the people, and that nobody, including lawmakers, law enforcement officials and judges, the president, governor, council Chairperson, or whatever the status, political, religious, traditional or military is exempted from being accountable to the law.

It also requires that no Nigerian should be victimized in the application of the law, either because she is a female, a poor person, from a particular ethnic group, religious group, or opposition political party.

This also requires that no authority must govern the people outside the provisions of the constitution.

But Mohammed Mustapha Akanbi,et al, on Rule of Law in Nigeria state "The rule of law is expected to be the guiding principle of governance since it is the foundation of good governance.

The experience in Nigeria is to the contrary as successive administration in the country often violated the concept with carelessness and recklessness."

Indeed, nearly all past governments in Nigeria, civil and military, have displayed varying degree of impunity and have records of rule of law breaches.

Nigerians have experienced outright suspension of the constitution, selective justice system, allegations of unconstitutional exercise of executive powers, infringement on human rights and press freedom, as well as legislative interferences, and more.

During the military years, it became a regular pattern for Nigerians to experience the suspension and modification of certain provisions of the constitution in an attempt to maintain power, legitimize the governments and to stifle dissenting voices.

Even though military interventions negates constitutionalism and the rule of law, the military always pretend to have come to promote the rule of law. "What is striking is the fact that on attaining power through the barrel of the gun as against the ballot box, the military junta usually proclaimed the rule of law as the corner stone of their administration." Fred Agbaje: (1995) The civilian governments in Nigeria, over the years, have also proven to have shown great intolerance to the principles of rule of law with high incidents of impunity, selective justice, executive high-handedness and wanton human rights abuses, to name a few.

Perhaps, these long years of disregard for rule of law in Nigeria has impacted negatively on the average citizen's behavior toward constitutionalism and the rule of law. For instance, even the basic right to fair hearing is frequently disregarded, or undermined.

There are several instances where citizens bribe the Police to put fellow citizens behind bars without trial as at when due. Another sad case in point is the recent mob lynching of one Talle Mai Ruwa, who was reportedly set ablaze in Bauchi, for allegedly blaspheming against Prophet Mohammed.

Yet, there's the need for Nigerians to embrace the rule of law at all levels for a more peaceful and just society.

Imperative of Nationwide Value Reorientation

The National Orientation Agency (NOA) has recently launched a nationwide campaign for moral reawakening in Nigeria. The project is intended to correct the obvious moral decay in the Nigerian society.

Indeed, Nigerian society of this era is fast losing the core values that have long molded its character, and shaped the behaviors and attitudes of the people.

Just recently, the National Drug Law Enforcement Agency (NDLEA) Chairman, retired Brig. General Buba Marwa, disclosed that Kano state has about two million drug addicts, representing 16 per cent prevalence. Marwa to Governor Abdullahi Ganduje, that "In Kano, drug abuse prevalence is 16 per cent; that is, in every six persons, one is a drug addict and they are between the ages of 15 and 64 years.

"Kano state has close to two million drug users abusing tramadol, codeine and other cough syrups, rather than cannabis."

According to the Global Cannabis Report and the Africa Hemp and Cannabis Report, in their 2019 industry outlook, Nigeria has the highest rate of cannabis use in the world with 20 million users.

The reports made available to Business Day, "indicate 19.4 per cent of Nigeria's population over the age of 15 consumed cannabis in the past year and at least 12 per cent consumed it monthly.

The newspaper notes "At number one position, Nigeria with 19.4 per cent of its population using cannabis is followed by Canada with 15.8 per cent, and in third position, the United States with 15 percent."

In a country that is considered a country of youths, this figure is high, and does not portend anything good.

This is because drug abuse is associated with criminality and all kinds of social vices, which include sexual immorality and prostitution. In an article Addressing Prostitution Concerns in Nigeria: Issue, Problems and Prospects, by E.E. Alobo and Rita Ndifon, "The practice of prostitution is at an alarming rate in Nigeria, it is seen as a deviant subculture in Nigeria and it is practiced by prostitutes in private homes, in brothels, and in hotels as an adaptation to poverty, unemployment and as a feasibility way for them to make money." The report estimates that "The number of juveniles engaging in prostitution is estimated at between 100,000 and 300,000 per year."

While a lot has been said about adult prostitution, which is seen as the oldest profession, child or juvenile prostitution is one that has not gained much attention despite its huge damaging implications.

It's very common, in recent years, to find young girls between 16 and 23 years, of school age, hanging out in pubs with hooker dresses, in search of male customers.

These youngsters are known to consume large doze of drugs, such as cannabis, codeine and shisha. Considering the large number of these young girls on the streets of Abuja, Lagos, Port harcourt, Benin, Asaba and other cities, the estimate given above is an obvious under estimation of the real figure.

This is disheartening and an indication of a loosening moral fabric of the Nigerian society.

Daily, the newspapers are agog with news of huge amount of money allegedly looted by young internet fraudsters, corporate executives and public servants across the country.

It is no longer a thing of shame to steal.

Social vices in Nigeria have assumed different dimension in more recent times with even parents encouraging, conspiring or conniving with the young. It is noted that the juvenile prostitutes are largely patronized by adults who see them as fun tools for sexual adventure.

While commenting on adult role in the decay of the educational system, Yomi Otubela, Founder of Yomi Otubela Foundation (YOF), spoke at a press conference ahead of the 2017 YOF scholarship examination saying "Until leaders and followers determine to make things change, that is when the sector will move forward.

The value system has eroded up to the extent that even parents do not know what standard education is all about "Parents are now aiding their children in all shades of examination malpractices. We have also seen schools compromising the standard of education in order to make more money."

No doubt, young people learn from the behaviors of adults and parents within their environment. So in this regard, the key institutions of family, schools, worship centers and tradition have significant roles to play in restoring the values that once distinguished Nigerians. Adults and parents in society cannot continue in immoral and corrupt practices and hope for disciplined generation of youth followers.

It is time to reorientate young people on positive values. Values influence the child's thinking, which in turn shapes relationship, behaviors, choices and sense of self-worth.

According to Lady Franca Orakwue, Executive Director, Positive Values Initiative International, "Positive values help young people avoid negative behaviors and also help guide their day-to-day actions and inactions.

Poverty Reduction in Nigeria

Nigeria is one of the countries in the world burdened with extreme poverty.

The problem of poverty in Nigeria has assumed the proportion that requires very urgent and tactical approach to bring the scourge to the barest minimum.

Successive governments have designed and implemented poverty eradication or reduction program with little impact on the lives of Nigeria's huge population. The scourge seems to defy much of government efforts when policy outcome is measured against huge government spending.

For instance, in recent years, under Good luck Jonathan Administration, Nigerian federal government invested trillions of naira in his Transformation agenda to reduce the effect of poverty on the people. The total projected investment for the 5 year plan, as presented by the Honourable Minister of National Planning, is N 35. 511. 29 trillion, and of this amount, the government was meant to provide 57. 10 percent or N 20. 277.72 trillion.

Yet, two years into the implementation of the plan, the World Bank in it's Nigeria Economic Report May 2013, claimed that poverty was still on increase, particularly in rural areas even though government report on macroeconomic outlook claimed to be improving.

Another report in the Guardian of May 7, 2013 puts it succinctly. It states that "While the economy is booming, precious little wealth trickles down to the poor."

Muhammadu Buhari Administration at inception appears to be confronting the issue of poverty by the transfer of cash to Nigerians through Market Money and other empowerment program. He has set an ambitious plan of lifting 100 million Nigerians out of poverty.

Already according to reports, the government claims to have lifted about 10. 5 million Nigerians out of poverty in the past two years, and a total of 12 million households with the past 5 years through the cash transfer program.

But analysts say Nigeria's poverty profile remains grim and embarrassing for a country endowed with humongous human and natural resources. The Nigerian National Bureau of Statistics said in 2020 that 40% or 83 million Nigerians live in poverty.

Although Nigeria's poverty profile for 2021 has not yet been released, it is estimated that the number of poor people will increase to 90 million, or 45% of the population, in 2022.

If the World Bank's income poverty threshold of $3.20 per day is used, Nigeria's poverty rate is 71%. Compared to lower rates for some oil-producing developing countries like Brazil (9.1%), Mexico (6.5%), Ecuador (9.7%) and Iran (3.1%), this is grim.

The Nigerian National Bureau of Statistics data suggest that the number of poor Nigerians exceeds the total population of South Africa, Namibia, Botswana, Lesotho, Mauritius and Eswatini combined. Stephen Onyeiwi (2021) Nigeria is home to an estimated 200 million in people who are mostly young and unemployed or underemployed. This reality poses a great danger for the country already encumbered with several social challenges. Many young people can be found on the streets begging for daily bread. Others are preoccupied with illegitimate activities, like internet fraud and armed robbery. Yet many others have resorted to gambling and sport betting.

Women and ladies on their part who are more vulnerable during such economic downturns, have unimaginable percentage of their population neck deep in prostitution. There are high number of young girls of school age, prostituting not only to feed themselves and their families, but also to finance their education. A UNICEF report on the Situation of Women and Children in Nigeria claims that "Nigeria's women of childbearing age (between 15 and 49 years of age) suffer disproportionally high level of health issues surrounding birth... While the country represents 2.4 percent of the world's population, it currently contributes 10 percent of global death."

Children are significant part of Nigeria's huge population and are also recipients of the trauma of the country's high poverty profile. The UNICEF report confirmed this stating that "While little over one in three of Nigeria's whole population lives below the poverty line, among children this proportion surges to 75 percent."

These go to show the complex and far reaching implications of poverty, and the urgent need to tackle the problems with required effectiveness. While there is need to address the problems concerning the education system, lack of access to quality healthcare, access to drinking water, and others, government needs to fund, or support the creation of much more jobs, particularly in agriculture and small scale manufacturing. But very urgent is the need to drive down market prices of food stuff to make it affordable to all.

Unemployment in Nigeria

Unemployment is one of Nigeria's most challenging development problems. It occurs when people who have actively sought for job opportunities in the past five years are unable to find jobs, according to International Labour Organization.

Unemployment can also occur when people lose their jobs to re-trenchment, business failure and so on, and when people, particularly the youths do not have any opportunity to work. Experts believe that unemployment arises where labor supply is higher than labor demand within an economy.

This is clearly the situation in Nigeria with the 2021 unemployment rate at 32.5 percent. Nwanguma, et al (2012), enumerated the causes of unemployment to include: rural – urban migration, rapid population growth, corruption, outdated school curriculum, leadership/managerial problems, poverty, lack of employable skills, increase in the supply of educated manpower, lack of adequate youth development programs.

Unemployment in Nigeria has increased the problems of youth restiveness, internet fraud, armed robbery, kidnapping, violent crimes, prostitution, drug addiction, cultism, gambling and more.

These days in many parts of this country, the youths are wasting their lives on alcohol, drug, sex and sport betting. While it has also become fashionable, in recent time to veil one's unemployment status with the 'self-employed' tag for social acceptability even though in reality no real business is in place.

Over the years, successive administrations have made efforts to solve the problem of unemployment but with little success. Between the administrations of Good luck Jonathan and Muhammadu Buhari, the N-Power program was put in place to generate employment for the teeming youth population.

The Muhammadu Buhari government has reportedly invested huge sum of money to create employment in the agriculture sector. Yet more effort is required.

Non Governmental Organizations in Nigeria have made significant contributions through empowerment schemes but these contributions are clearly not sufficient.

Greater outcomes can be achieved with better collaborative approach between all levels of government, non profit organizations and the private sector.

But such collaborations need to be complemented with value reorientation program that redefines what Nigerian youths think employment to mean.

At independence, Nigerians inherited a culture of the white collar job that promoted the class system, and undermines all other job types. Everyone chased after office jobs and also encouraged their children and loved ones to do same.

Suddenly, no one wanted any job other than the white collar job. Crafts and apprenticeship were soon relegated.

The educational system was also modelled to produce knowledgeable graduates without skills to confront and survive the challenges of the emerging world. Up till now, in spite of global changes with their ever disruptive technologies, few changes have occurred in the educational system, and the thinking of Nigeria's youths has remained the same.

Joe Biden, President of the United States of America is currently dealing with the same issue of unemployment, and has recently unfolded his plans. In his speech to Americans, Biden warned that anyone who rejects a job would lose the unemployment benefits.

Biden also sought to create more blue collar job opportunities to meet job target.

In Nigeria the federal, state and local governments can encourage Nigerians to accept job opportunities outside the white collar jobs. Nigerians need to relearn the concept of labor. There's dignity in labor and no job is to be considered more superior over another as long as the job provides for individual needs.

In most multinational corporations in Nigeria, every job is important, and the worker is treated with respect in spite of job title. In some, it's even forbidden to ridicule or harass anyone on the basis of job title.

Entrepreneurship is another instrument to reduce unemployment in Nigeria. Countries like China, Japan, for example, show clearly how citizens can build wealth and create massive employment through entrepreneurship.

Today, big global brands were grown through the entrepreneurial prowess of founders through the support of their governments.

However, citizens need to help the situation by availing themselves of the various learning opportunities to develop competence in this digital age.

High rate of unemployment in Nigeria is unacceptable, and every stakeholder must be involved in finding solutions.

Life Expectancy in Nigeria

In the four years, life expectancy in Nigeria has been on the increase, according to data presented by Macrotrends, an interactive chart of global stock, bond, commodity and real estate markets that also include key economic and demographic indicators.

In 2018, life expectancy was 54.18 years with a 0.83 percent increase from 2017.

This figure, 2019, rose to 54.49 years indicating an increase of 0.58 percent. In 2020, there was further increase by 0.59 percent to 54.81 years, and for the year 2021, life expectancy is projected at 55.12 years showing a further increase by 0.57 percent.

However, addressing a press conference in March 2021, Dr. Iyke Odo, President of the Association of General and Private Medical Practitioners of Nigeria, put the current life expectancy at 54 years contrary to 55.12 years projection.

This figure by the doctors's association, brings Nigeria below some African countries such as Togo, Ghana and South Africa in the life expectancy index.

On what the life expectancy means for Nigeria, the association's President queried "On the average, how long are you expected to live as a Nigerian, given the life support, welfare system available, the quality of life, cost of living, given the leadership, environment and all that around an average Nigerian?

"You are expected to live for 54 years. And if you are more than 54, it means you have broken the jinx. You have defied Nigeria to survive more than it expects you to survive or live."

Concern for low life expectancy in Nigeria has been growing for decades since the turn around of Nigeria's economic fortunes.

In the 70s and up to early 80s, Nigeria had a near stable economy and a robust healthcare system that attracted medical tourists from countries like, Ghana, South Africa, India and Saudi Arabia.

But today, Nigerian medical tourists reportedly spent N 500 billion for treatment in foreign countries.

Experts have attributed Nigeria's low life expectancy to a range of factors, including high unemployment rate, Poor health, poverty, deaths from preventable causes, illiteracy, high corruption.

Dr. John Ahukannah, Abia State Commissioner for Health, in a 2018 presentation entitled: Improving Life Expectancy in Africa, as reported by Vanguard newspaper of April 3, 2018, citing a countryspecific polling service, NOIPolls, noted other causes of low life expectancy in Nigeria and Africa to include: motor accident (16 percent), natural death (6 percent), stress (5 percent), high blood pressure (5 percent), poor medical care (3 percent), bad lifestyle (2 percent), high cost of living (2 percent), crime (5 percent), negligence (5 percent), and others (7 percent).

In recent years, economic hardship accelerated by high inflation rate and rising rate of unemployment in the country has placed millions of Nigerians at risk of stress, high blood pressure and early deaths.

The Guardian newspaper of 17 May 2021, reported that 76.2 million of Nigerians, which is 38.1 percent prevalence are hypertensive while only about 23 million are on treatment. Poverty and anxiety raise the risk of hypertension that is well-being known cause of early death.

On number of deaths from preventable deceases, Nigeria had the highest number of global malaria deaths (23 percent) in 2019, according to the 2020 World Malaria Report.

Road Traffic Accident is a major cause of deaths in the country due to poor roads, and other factors such as drug and alcohol abuse, fatigue and more. A Sunday Vanguard report of February 20, 2020, claimed that 41,257 people died in road accidents in 97 months, as the country loses 15 persons per day, 4 persons every six hours. In 2020, the report estimated from combined data from Federal Road Safety

Commission and the Nigeria Bureau of Statistics, that not less than 4,918 deaths were recorded from road traffic accidents in Nigeria.

High level of insecurity in the country is also impacting on life expectancy of Nigerians. A 2018 report on violent deaths affirmed this. Nigeria-Watch: Eighth Report on Violence 2018 was published with the support of the French Institute for Research in Africa. The report states that "There was a 1.4 percent increase in the number of violent deaths in Nigeria in 2018. Fatalities increased from 10,515 in 2017 to 10,665 in 2018."

The main causes of violent deaths in Nigeria, according to the report were crime, political issues, land issues, religious issues, cattle grazing and road accidents. The report further states "Boko Haram conflicts killed 2,135 in 2018 less than the 2,829 fatalities in 2017, accounting for 28 percent decrease. Cult related killings accounted for 453 deaths in 162 incidents, while 238 people were killed in 350 lethal incidents involving security operatives.

Experts have also linked a country's education level to its level of life expectancy because education, they say, augments labor market productivity and income growth. John Ahukannah (2018). But unfortunately, Nigeria has a poor literacy profile. Nearly half the population cannot read and write.

Life expectancy in the country cannot improve significantly without addressing the key issues like, healthcare funding/delivery policies, improved education, road construction/ rehabilitation, employment creation, effective security, and more.

But most importantly, good governance is crucial for the realization of quality life, and well-being for improved life expectancy of Nigerians.

Impediments to Maternal Mortality

Ignorance and perceptual factors have been observed as main impediments to maternal mortality reduction in Nigeria.

A UNICEF report on the Situation of Women and Children in Nigeria claims there are over 40 million women of childbearing age (between 15 and 49 years of age) in Nigeria, while the country contributes 10 percent of global deaths for pregnant mothers.

According to the report: "Latest figures show a maternal mortality rate of 576 per 1000 births, the fourth highest on Earth." Yet, a World Health Organization's document published in September 2019, gave an estimate of 814 per 1000 livebirths, and listed lack of information and cultural beliefs and practices as part of the main factors that prevent women from receiving or seeking care during pregnancy and childbirth, and advised thus: "To improve maternal health, barriers that limit access to quality maternal health services must be identified and addressed at both health system and societal levels."

While the mandate to address the issue of quality maternal health services in the country lies with the various tiers of government, the other important issue of promoting change of attitudes and perceptions by women and their family members within the society need to be given attention.

This is because much of the factors that have inspired negative public perception on maternal care services can be eliminated through quality information dissemination.

Uncertain about the quality of maternal care available in authorized healthcare centers does affect decision making during pregnancy and childbirth. At such point, many women opt for traditional alternative with its associated risks, rather than submit to highly skilled medical services available at maternal health centers.

Some experts note that even if the standard of services in Nigeria primary, secondary or tertiary health facilities is improved, maternal mortality may still be high.

Most times, the choices that these women make in the utilization of a health facility are based on their perception of care, and not on the actual quality of care being delivered. Ope B.W (2020).

To further buttress this point, Ope cited some examples based on earlier surveys. "In Ota, Ogun State, Southwest Nigeria, for instance, several women believe that delivering in a noninstitutional setting is better than in a modern facility because traditional birth attendants show more concern than skilled birth attendants.

Similarly, in Northern Nigeria, Puddah (female isolation) is very common, where women are isolated and encouraged to give birth at home.

Many in these settings believe that allowing an outsider help with delivery could be disrespectful.

In Giwa Local Government Area (LGA) of Kaduna State Nigeria, despite living close to a health facility with free maternal health services, majority of the women were not utilizing the facility for child delivery.

In Esan and Etsako LGAs of Edo State Nigeria, some authors reported that perception of maternal healthcare quality plays a major role in the use of health services, with 25 percent of women, which is perhaps under – reported in that community, delivering at home even when a primary healthcare facility is located close to where the women reside.

Ope also noted an outcome of a study of the same LGAs in Edo State, which revealed that some women prefer traditional birth attendants to primary healthcare providers because "the former are friendlier (similar to the experience at Ota), and offer native medicine (traditional herbs), which is believed to be the best form of medication during childbirth."

These study outcomes, no doubt, reinforce the position that availability of quality and affordable maternal care centers alone do not translate to utilization of such facilities by the women.

Information and orientation are important tools that can be deployed to drive positive change of attitudes and behaviors.

To reduce the rate of maternal mortality in Nigeria, particularly in the rural parts of the country, it may be pertinent to systematically engage households, especially the women and young girls, in a penetrating orientation campaign, to provide the relevant information that can change negative perceptions and attitudes toward maternal healthcare services.

In fact, Ope noted that "a woman's perception of 'quality care' might even influence another person's health–seeking behavior.

For instance, if a woman's experience of care during a normal delivery was negative, other women whom she might have told of such experience might delay in deciding to seek care (even when standard quality services are provided at the health facility), thereby increasing the likelihood of birth complications and maternal deaths.

Therefore, a holistic approach to maternal mortality reduction in Nigeria is necessary, and should be pursued with vigor by all relevant stakeholders.

Safe Schooling for Nigerian Child

It has become increasingly evident that the overall prosperity of any nation is largely defined by its health profile, just as improved child safety system is fundamental for its social progress.

Yet since over six decades of Nigeria's independence in 1960, successive governments have done little to evolve standardized safe-schooling program to enhance the quality of child education for its teeming young population.

Nearly half the 200 million population, 46 percent, currently under the age of 15, are constantly at the risk of suffering several safety incidents that often lead to severe injuries, that in some cases, keep them out of the classrooms, which is not acceptable to global health authorities.

A research result on High rate of injuries among students in Southern Nigeria: An urgent call to action, published in 2013 noted that "Homes and schools were settings injuries occurred mostly.

Over 68% of the reported injuries were unintentional. On the average, 2 days of normal school activity were lost per injured persons because of an injury."

Traffic injuries, falls, animal and reptile bites are some of the named causes.

The Nigerian child is still confronted with insufficient, obsolete and at-risk learning infrastructure, a situation that continues to endanger their survival in schools.

One report published by United Nation Children Education Fund (UNICEF), regrets that "..the child – friendly school concept, which UNICEF is advocating for, is not comprehensively adopted by various states in Nigeria"

The global body in the report decries the hazardous learning environment which the Nigerian child daily contends with, while pointing to the millions of children sometimes packed in hundreds in dilapidated buildings, and at other times under trees.

In another report published in 2017, UNICEF stated that, "The national legal framework for child protection is the Child Rights Act 2003, but to date, only 23 of 36 states have adopted the Act... A national survey in 2014 found that 6 out of 10 children reported having suffered one or more forms of violence before reaching 18 years of age, with 70 percent of those experiencing multiple incidents of violence."

Most of these children, of course, are under 15 years of age with nearly 31 million under the age of 5.

Conditions facing the Nigerian school child can best be described as precarious.

At homes and in schools, millions of these children learn and play in rough and sometimes hazardous terrains, placing many at risk. The insufficiency or unavailability of preventive measures, and functional safe-schooling facilities also increases the risks for the children.

In Nigeria today, available record indicate that there are more than 544,434 public primary schools as well as 14,258 post primary schools. Although some progress has been made by some state governments, attainment of totally conducive and safe learning environment in the country's public schools remains a far cry.

Investigation has revealed that children who feel unsafe at school perform worse academically. Meanwhile, accidents and violence have always occurred in schools involving children.

The UNICEF report showed from a 2014 nationwide survey that 6 out of 10 children reported having suffered one or more forms of violence before reaching 18. Some of such violence most likely occurred within the school environment.

Globally a sharp increase in incidents of juvenile violence has been reported, meaning that child protection should also be prioritized in schools.

It has therefore become increasingly important to provide, in addition to incidents and injury preventive measures, some safety facilities like, the first aid kits for timely interventions in our schools.

Such measures in schools will certainly reduce the statistics of children that suffer serious health conditions arising from minor and major accidents, and from other incidents requiring urgent attention.

Parents and guardians at home need to also pay special attention to children while they are at home.

At homes, children suffer injuries from unintentional incidents, and these injuries can become fatal enough to deprive them from returning to school as at when due.

But, most importantly, there is the need for children, teachers and parents to be adequately educated on standard safety practices both at homes and in schools to help children of school age learn and play safely.

Addressing Out-of-School Crisis in Nigeria

Saturday 25, September 2021, the reubenabati. com.ng, published a report on Former Emir of Kano, Muhammad Sanusi's warning concerning Nigeria's uncertain economy, and it's reluctance to commit to developing a knowledge based society.

Bemoaning the country's poor investment in education and innovation, Sanusi reportedly noted that: "Countries like Kenya, Rwanda and Senegal are ahead of us. I am not even talking about South Africa.

Our expenditure on education is only seven per cent of the

budget. We are spending less on education than Ghana; I am not talking about as per the percentage of the budget; in absolute terms, even though the Ghanaian economy is much smaller than the Nigerian economy, even though the Ghanaian government revenue is less than Nigerian revenue.

Ghana is spending more on education than Nigeria.

"And we are surprised that Industries are moving to Ghana. We are surprised that the Ghanaian President has become the leading President in Africa?

We are not investing in education and human capital."

There has been series of conversations in the country for some years now around the subject of budgetary allocations to adequately finance Nigeria's educational system in order to boost the sector, generally.

So, Sanusi's recent outburst is coming to reinforce the need for objective review of the national education policy in the face of shaming indices.

In January 2021, the Vanguard newspaper reported that the president of National Association of Nigerian Students (NANS), Comrade Sunday Asefon, accused the federal government of not being serious in the effort to revitalize the education sector. Asefon said that "The 2021 budget allocation for the education sector is worst in a decade.

We call on FG to find means to jack up the education budget. We also urge the government to call for an education summit for stakeholders to come together and find a lasting solution to the challenges facing the sector. Nigeria should follow the path Singapore followed to tackle its education challenge and look forward to having a knowledge base education."

When analyzed, Nigeria budgeted 6.3 per cent of its 2021 national budget on the Federal Ministry of Education. A sum of N742.5 billion out of the total N11.7 trillion budget was allowed to the ministry out of which N615.1 billion is proposed to go into the recurrent expenditure of the ministry covering personnel and overhead costs while N127.3 billion is devoted to capital expenditure, the newspaper reported.

Nigeria currently has the world's highest Out-of-school figure. According to a 2018 UNICEF report, Nigeria's Out-of-school figure has risen from 10.5 million to 13.2 million, which is the highest in the world.

The UNICEF survey further states that there are also huge number in children in school, but who are learning nothing. There's, however, a conflicting report of the current figure from another source that quoted the Federal Ministry of Education, which puts the current Out-of-school figure at 10. 5 million officially indicating a 3 million increase from last year.

This conflict, notwithstanding, Nigeria's huge Out-of-school population does not augur well for a nation that prides itself as the giant of the African continent.

Nigeria's estimated 200 million population with nearly half the population under 15, which is the school age, means that the country has huge responsibility to address this deficiency.

Budgetary allocations to child education, particularly, need to be reviewed and upgraded to accommodate the acquisition of relevant facilities and infrastructures, especially in the most impoverished parts of the country.

Cultural considerations have also been noted to diminish the prospect of improved schooling in the northern part of Nigeria.

The government needs to properly engage key stakeholders to deal with the problem, so that children can be put back in schools.

The Minister of State, Education, Chukwuemeka Nwajiuba, recently acknowledged the country's pathetic education profile, during the inauguration of "Better Education Service Delivery for All (BESDA), when he noted that new current challenges confronting the education system have left much to be desired, and include high illiteracy level, infrastructural decay and deficits, according to the News Agency of Nigeria (NAN).

There are several other reasons for Nigeria's poor Out-of-school figure but none is beyond redemption.

Political will is critical if Nigeria must make significant progress.

Dangers of Arms Proliferation in Nigeria

Proliferation of illegal fire arms and light weapons is evidently undermining the nation's internal security.

This fact was recently corroborated by a report on Small Arms, Mass Atrocities and Migration in Nigeria, published in October by SBM Intelligence.

The report claims that proliferation of small arms and ammunition's is driving increased rate of violence, rise of armed groups, which has led to fatalities and displacement of several Nigerians. A Daily Trust report of February 26, 2020, also stated that:

"The worsening insecurity in Nigeria, manifested in terrorist attacks, banditry, kidnapping, communal clashes, violent crimes, cult wars, ethnic and regional militias, and the like, provide enough evidence that small and illicit arms are in circulation in abundance.

On the other hand, the acquisition of small arms through illegal means is being done by Nigerians to ensure self-help against violent acts because the nation's security infrastructure seems to have been overwhelmed."

No doubt, the increase in the number of illegal firearms is fueling increase in violent crimes and armed conflicts in the country.

In more recent years, these violent crimes have taken to new dimension and sophistication in the way they are executed.

Few months ago, marked the beginning of a new trend, of a series of attacks on correctional centers and police headquarters. Dare-devil bandits are on rampage across Nigeria, which places the average law abiding citizens at risk.

According to a further investigation published on August 24, 2021 by Daily Trust, "Villagers in Niger, Zamfara, Kaduna, Plateau and Katsina States are on the lead as many communities in States having security challenges have stockpiled assault rifles to protect themselves."

Many citizens in these crises-ridden parts of Nigeria no longer trust their governments enough to protect them, so they would rather resort to self-help.

In Nigeria, the firearms law requires only security personnel and licensed individuals to possess specified firearms. Yet, the SBM report has revealed that: "The number of small arms in circulation in Nigeria, in the hands of civilian non-state actors is estimated at 6, 145, 000." This number is staggering and dangerous for a country that is already on the edge.

Many analysts have blamed the authorities at the Nigerian borders for seemingly compromising, and leaving the borders open for illicit trades.

But these are more allegations since no official has been prosecuted so far. But the concern to reduce firearms and light weapons is not just a Nigerian issue. It's a global problem.

They must involve the ECOWAS and the United Nations bodies because the world cannot afford a Nigeria that is crises ridden at this time.

Gender Violation and Abuse

A retrospective peep through the crevice of Nigeria's chequered cultural, political and socio economic history would reveal a long disheartening tale of inequalities, gender discrimination, violence and wanton abuses; tales of unending struggle against systemic deprivations, and suppressed freedoms and choices.

Yet, like in many developing countries women, and the girl child in Nigeria, continues to struggle for survival, and to thrive with undiminished fervor.

Despite numerous treacherous challenges from retrogressive traditional beliefs and practices, large scale poverty, ethnic and religious conflicts, threat of war, rights abuses, inequalities and exclusions, among others, there's increasing evidence of several advancements recorded by Nigerian women in many aspects of their national life.

In academics, politics, business and the professions, these women even though abysmally disproportional to men, have continued to push through the odds to support themselves, families, to contribute to nation building.

But this sharp improvement in the state of Nigerian women did not just occur. Since 1990, when the Federal Ministry of Women Affairs and Social Development, which was established along with the 36 state ministries, there have been evidence of progressive measures deliberately taken to ensure better living conditions for women and the girl child in Nigeria.

Subsequent adoption and commitment to Beiging Declaration and Platform for Action, a blueprint for advancement of women rights launched on September 15, 1995, no doubt, also accelerated the change seen today.

There're also many important actions taken by the federal ministry of women affairs and social development partnering organizations that have greatly impacted on women and their children, particularly the girl child, including:

-Launch of the National Strategies To End Child Marriage in Nigeria by 2030.

-Adoption in 2006 and 2007 of a National Gender Policy and its strategic implementation Framework and Plan

-Impressive poverty Reduction Strategies and Programmes

-Improved girl child enrollment in primary and secondary schools.

-Substantial improvement of maternal mortality.

But in spite of these achievements, the lives of women and the girl child need to be improved upon in Nigeria. A recent report by the United Nations Children Education Funds on condition of women in Nigeria, revealed that: "Nigeria's 40 million women of child bearing age (between 15 and 49 years of age) suffer a disproportional high level of health issues surrounding birth.

Another UNICEF noted in 2017, that "Nigerian children are vulnerable to a wide range of abuses and harmful traditional practices.

The national legal framework for child protection is the Child Rights Act 2003, but to date, only 23 of 36 states have adopted the Act.

"On implementation, the report says "Implementation is patchy with many local authority bodies unaware of their duties under the law.

The recent nationwide rise in violence and insecurity has further increased the risk of women and girls. The situation not only subjects young girls and female teachers to several shades of violence and molestation.

It does, in fact threatens the children's school attendance. Research has shown children who feel unsafe at school perform worse academically.

In northern Nigeria where kidnapping of school children and teachers have been rampant, in recent time, schools have been reportedly shut, and children no longer go to school.

These reported attacks have been deadly, with hundreds of young girls abducted for months. Few years ago, the notorious Boko Haram and the bandits, began to target schools for their nefarious activities. Lives of the Nigerian girl child have been greatly endangered ever since.

Young women in Nigeria has also been subject to violent attacks through rapes by armed robbers and other criminals.

Although Nigeria is not the only country where women and girls are violated and abused; countries like South Africa and the United States still command high percentage.

But the governments, both federal and states, must step up to ensure safety for the women.

Infant Mortality

Since the commencement of the Fourth Republic, there have been series of policies and actions to strengthen the health sector in Nigeria.

Unlike the years before, the Nigerian health sector began to experience a new commitment to improved healthcare delivery.

However, many observers have maintained that successive governments have not made much progress judging by available key indices, such as: life expectancy, maternal mortality ratio (MMR), infant mortality rate and others.

For instance, in 2020, infant mortality in Nigeria was 59.181 deaths per 1000 live births, which improved by 2.5 percent to the current infant mortality rate for Nigeria in 2021 at 57.701 deaths per 1000 live births, a 2.5% decline from 2020.

This figure is however still considered high. Critics insist the current figure does not only reflect the abysmally low budgetary allocations to the health sector, but also does reflect the poor socio–economic realities in the country.

Poor infrastructures and facilities, lack of power, drinkable water, widespread hunger and poverty, high level illiteracy, corruption, cultural and religious constraints, all combine to endanger the life of new born and under five infants.

According to A. A. O. Olaniyi, etal, "Nigeria's newborn mortality is among the highest in the world. It was estimated that 10% of all newborn deaths in the world happened in Nigeria.

The country was ranked 11th highest on newborn deaths in the world." Under five mortality is by no means lesser. The UNICEF country data estimates Nigeria under five mortality at 117.2 deaths per 1000 live births.

Experts attributed the specific causes of infant mortality in Nigeria to include: prematurity, intrapartum complication, birth asphyxia, infections, etc.

Efforts to reduce these preventable deaths, and to further reduce the nation's infant mortality figures, according to Olaniyi, should involve improving access to skilled health professionals during pregnancy and the time of birth as well as other lifesaving interventions like immunization against illnesses, breastfeeding, increase access to clean water and good sanitation, although these are currently beyond the reach of the world poorest communities and other public health measure.

There has been regular advocacy to push up the health sector budgetary allocations to make funds more readily available for upgrade of infrastructures and facilities in the sector, especially to improve the primary and secondary health care services. Such increase, no doubt, is desirable, because Nigeria current spending on health is very dismal compare to some countries within the region.

In 2009, the Obasanjo administration established the Nigeria Midwife Service Scheme (MSS) "to help reduce maternal and infant mortality rates in rural and under served areas of the country.

The scheme was to address the shortage of skilled obstetric care providers and poor access to basic emergency obstetric care by employing and deploying newly qualified, unemployed and retired midwives, and equipping clinics…", an official report states. Phase one of the MSS occurred in about 652 primary care clinics across the country's 36 States to reach and serve about 10 million people.

Such highly targeted investment was crucial to help those in rural areas. But there should be consistent investment in the health sector to change the narrative.

Millions of expectant and nursing mothers live amongst Nigeria's extremely poor population in the rural parts of the country. These women are daily confronted with several poverty related challenges such as hunger and malnutrition.

Continued interest and reliance of traditional health centers in these parts have contributed to much of the risks facing Children and their mothers. These mothers seem to trust the maternal care offered by these centers.

Recent surveys have indicated that most of these mothers feel the government registered centers do not show adequate care. So it becomes discouraging for the women to submit and register for maternal care during pregnancy and child delivery.

Religious and cultural constraints have long influenced decisions in the country. In the northern part of Nigeria, women prefer the traditional centers to government approved maternal care centers because their culture discourage women from submitting to strangers outside the family.

Low level of knowledge amongst women in the rural area are also contributing factors.

Education and knowledge can prepare mothers to provide proper care for Children.

The overall implication is that these women and their unborn or new born babies do not receive the proper care required to grow healthy or overcome the initial health challenges.

Therefore, in addition to seeking to increase the budgetary allocations to the health sector, governments need to do more to improve the socio economic environment.

This is crucial for the country with over 200 million population. Nearly half Nigeria's population is notably illiterate and more inclined to religious and cultural dictates. The authorities need to show visible commitment toward the general health of Nigerians, men, women and children alike.

REFERENCES

Adeleye, Bode. 2000. *Policy Making in Nigeria.* Lagos: Lorell Publishers.

Adejumobi, S. 1998. "Election in Africa Development: a fading of Democracy." *African Journals:* African Development. COSDESRIA, VOLXX.

Ajayi, D. D. 1999. *Crisis in Nigeria.* Ibadan: University Press.

Akindele. 2011. *Democracy in Nigeria.* Ibadan: Ilesanmi Press.

Kuwait Chapter of Arabian Journal of Business and Management Review. 2012. Vol. 1, no. 9 (May): 130.

Bayomi. 2011. *Nigerian Fourth Republic.* London: Stevenson Publishers Limited.

Borishade, Deji O. 2000. *Democratic Transitions in Nigeria.* Lagos: Henshaw Publishers.

Chikelue, O. K. 2011. *Political Governance in Post-independent Nigeria.* Enugu: Cripils Investments.

2009. "Democracy: The Second Liberation." *Africa Report,* Nov/Dec.

Dike, Victor. 2011. *Leadership, Democracy, and the Nigeria Economy: Lesson from the Past and Directions for the Future.* The Lightning Press, Sacramento 1999.

Dike, Victor. 2011). "The philosophy of Transforming Nigeria into a Corruption-free Society: Are the probes the Solution?" Online: www.nigeria-world.com, October 6, 1999.

Emma Obiasi, C. Nkwam Umaoma & Co. 2004. *Citizenship Education for Nigerian students in tertiary Education.* Owerri Imo

State Nigeria: New Vision Publishers.

Golden, P. C. 2010. *Fundamentals of Democracy.* London: Oxford University Press.

Hassan, C. C. 2009. *Current Issues in Nigerian Government and Politics.* Ibadan: University Press.

Igboanugo, Sunny. 200. "Kaduna riot is political, says Ojukwu." *The Guardian Online.* February 29, 2000.

Jakande, Y. K. 2008. *The Nigerian Legislature.* Lagos: Progressive Publishers.

Mamudu K. G. & Hassan, L. W. 2011. *Legitimacy in Governance.* Ibadan: Yolani Press.

National Bureau of Statistics Records. Abuja.

Nigeria's 2011 General Election Verdict. Posted by admin on May 28, 2011.

Odukoya, A. A. 2008. *The Making of a Political Leader.* Ibadan: Ibadan Press.

Ogbonna, Williams. 2005. *Military Rule in Nigeria.* Ibadan: Ilessanmi Press.

Ogundele, A. T. 2006. *The Fragmented Nigeria.* London: Oxford University Press.

Ogunkoya, Ademola. 2008. *The Principles of Democracy.* France: Luxembre Press.

Ojo, A. F. 1998. *Nigeria Again.* London: Oxford University Press.

Kuwait Chapter of Arabian Journal of Business and Management Review. 2012. Vol. 1, No.9 (May): 131.

Okafor, Celestine et al. 2000. "Verdict on Democracy 2000: We've failed woefully." *The Vanguard Online.* December 23, 2000.

Okafor, Gerald. 2011. *Political Administration in Nigeria: An Overview.* London: University Press.

Okebukola, Jide R. 2009. *The Dividends of Democracy.* London: Oxford University Press.

Okongwu, J. D. 1999. *The Era of the Fourth Republic in Nigeria.* Lagos: Olu Press.

Olugbenga, G. L. 2008. *Political Crises in Nigeria: Which Way Forward?* London: Oxford University Press.

Osagie, G. C. 2006. *Humanitarian Issues in Nigerian-Biafran Civil War.* Abuja: Saggas Press.

Oseloka, T. S. Y. 1994. *We Can Never Be the Same Again.* Washington: Afrique de Forthright.

Usman, D. O. 2010. *The Return of Civilian Rule.* Ogun: Ogunshoya Publishers.

Declaration of Rights. February 13, 1689.

House of Commons Information Office. http:// www.parliament.uk

House of Parliament. http://www.parliament.uk

Governor Fob James. 1995. "Separation of Powers—The Cornerstone of American Democracy." Delivered at the American Legislature Council. August 1995. http://www.positive atheism.org/writ/jamesalec.htm.

Bard, Vanessa and Mark Hurtwitz. Can the Supreme Court Ã¢,¬Å"Go PublicÃ¢,¬ ? The influence of the Supreme Court on congress. http://www. unpan.org/information/technical highlights/participants.htm

Parliamentary Supremacy, Judicial independence. Latimer House Guidelines for the Commonwealth. June 19, 1998.

Rules of Proceedings of the House of Representatives 1999–2003.

Constitution of the Federal Republic of Nigeria. 1999.

Paper presented at Capacity Building Retreat for Forum for Democracy and Good Governance at Confluence Hotel Lokoja, Kogi State. September 5–6, 2004.

Constitution of the Federal Republic of Nigeria. 1999.

E. Michael Joye and Kingsley Igweike. *Introduction to the 1979 Nigerian Constitution.*

Prof. Nwabueze. *Redefining the Nigerian Budget Process.*

Prof. Alex Gboyega. *Legislatures in a Presidential Democracy: An Overview.*

Columbia University. 1966. *State Legislatures in American Politics.*

Norman Ornstein. *The Role of the Legislature in a Democracy.*

Hood Philips: Constitutional and Administrative Law 7th Edition

Luce: Legislative Assemblies, 1924.

James Ojiako. *1st Four Years of Nigeria Executive Presidency, Success or Failure*

Lecky: Democracy and Liberty.

Prof. Elaigwu. 1999. "Transition to Transition." *NIALS Mirror.* Vol. 4, No.3 (December).

Vanguard Newspapers. July 22, 2012.

ABOUT THE
AUTHOR

Kemdi Chino Opara, the first of eleven (11) children, was born on January 21, 1960, to Chief (Sir) Louis O. Opara, the former general manager of Irvin and Burner Impress Account of the then Eastern Region of Nigeria and Chief (Lady) Christiana C. Opara of Umuchoke, Obazu-Mbieri, in Mbaitoli Local Government Area of Imo State. He found love in the home of late Barrister Christopher O. Nwarache, the former director of Foreign Exchange Control, Central Bank of Nigeria, and Mrs. Clara C. Nwarache of Ibusa in Delta State. His marriage to their first daughter, former Miss Angela Nneka Nwarache, a registered nurse practitioner by profession and an international relations analyst with focus in the Middle East countries, is blessed with a son and three daughters, all graduates of Howard University, Washington, DC, USA.

Kemdi Chino Opara started his education journey from Government Secondary School in Owerri, Imo State, Nigeria, after which he moved to the United States of America (USA). He continued his studies at the College of New Jersey in Ewing Township, New Jersey, to obtain a bachelor of science in industrial engineering. His postgraduate studies, consisting of two masters in business administration (MBA), include one in finance and the other in marketing research as well as a doctorate in education and social policy were obtained from Morgan State University, Baltimore, Maryland, USA.

Following his graduation, he served as an adjunct faculty member at the College of New Jersey in Ewing Township, New Jersey, in the area of business and economic statistics. He also worked for several years in the New York State Office of Mental Health where he assumed several top-level executive management positions. He retired from active service in government after twenty-one years.

He is a prolific writer with several publications to his name, including three authored books titled *The National Assembly Federal Republic of Nigeria: What You Should Know and Why?*, *The Man and His Destiny*, *Several volumes of The Journals: An X-ray of the Burning Issues in Nigeria and the Way Forward.* These publications are available both locally and internationally as well as on Amazon.com and other online outlets. In addition, he is a guest columnist on several print and online media outlets.

Kemdi Chino Opara has founded as well as cofounded several active companies in the USA. Locally, he is the founder and chairman of Kemdi Chino Opara Foundation (KCOF) and chairman/ CEO of GistAgrica Empowerment Foundation. The overall mission of these foundations is to give a flame of hope to the poor, the sick, and the needy. He is also an active member of several organizations including American Management Association, Institute of Industrial Engineers, National Fire Protection Association, all in the USA, and Kappa Delta Pi International Honor Society in Education, all geared toward uplifting humanity. In recognition of his humanitarian works, Kemdi Chino Opara has been honored with several awards and accolades both locally and internationally.

Kemdi Chino Opara is presently one of the directors of Opara dynasty company, Opara Industries Limited, and had served well in the past in several capacities including as a board member of World Igbo Congress (USA), as a member of Igwebuike Social Club in New Jersey, and as a Certified Code Enforcement Officer (USA). He would like to continue to serve and give back to humanity through the position of a senator, representing Owerri senatorial zone of Imo State, Nigeria.

Kemdi Chino Opara can best be described as empathic, an achiever, a prolific writer, a philanthropist, an astute politician, and a business mogul with a knack for excellence.

Printed in the USA
CPSIA information can be obtained
at www.ICGtesting.com
LVHW041632120424
777089LV00001B/29